Terence
Hawkes

Structuralism and Semiotics

Routledge
Taylor & Francis Group

LONDON AND NEW YORK

To ANN, as ever

First published 1977 by Methuen & Co. Ltd
Reprinted twice
Reprinted 1983 with revised bibliography
Reprinted three times

Reprinted 1991, 1992, 1997, 2003
by Routledge
2 Park Square, Milton Park, Abingdon, Oxford OX14 4RN

Second edition first published 2003
Reprinted 2005, 2006

Simultaneously published in the USA and Canada
by Routledge
270 Madison Ave, New York, NY10016

Routledge is an imprint of the Taylor & Francis Group, an informa business

© 1977, 2003 Terence Hawkes

Typeset in Joanna by RefineCatch Ltd, Bungay, Suffolk
Printed and bound in Great Britain by
TJ International Ltd, Padstow, Cornwall

British Library Cataloguing in Publication Data
A catalogue record for this book is available from the British Library

Library of Congress Cataloging in Publication Data
A catalog record for this book has been requested

ISBN10: 0–415–32152–2 (hbk)
ISBN10: 0–415–32153–0 (pbk)

ISBN13: 978–0–415–32152–5 (hbk)
ISBN13: 978–0–415–32153–2 (pbk)

CONTENTS

GENERAL EDITOR'S PREFACE

No doubt a third General Editor's Preface to *New Accents* seems hard to justify. What is there left to say? Twenty-five years ago, the series began with a very clear purpose. Its major concern was the newly perplexed world of academic literary studies, where hectic monsters called 'Theory', 'Linguistics' and 'Politics' ranged. In particular, it aimed itself at those undergraduates or beginning postgraduate students who were either learning to come to terms with the new developments or were being sternly warned against them.

New Accents deliberately took sides. Thus the first Preface spoke darkly, in 1977, of 'a time of rapid and radical social change', of the 'erosion of the assumptions and presuppositions' central to the study of literature. 'Modes and categories inherited from the past' it announced, 'no longer seem to fit the reality experienced by a new generation'. The aim of each volume would be to 'encourage rather than resist the process of change' by combining nuts-and-bolts exposition of new ideas with clear and detailed explanation of related conceptual developments. If mystification (or downright demonisation) was the enemy, lucidity (with a nod to the compromises inevitably at stake there) became a friend. If a 'distinctive discourse of the future' beckoned, we wanted at least to be able to understand it.

With the apocalypse duly noted, the second Preface proceeded piously to fret over the nature of whatever rough beast might stagger portentously from the rubble. 'How can we recognise or deal with the new?', it complained, reporting nevertheless the dismaying advance of 'a host of barely respectable activities for which we have no reassuring names' and promising a programme of wary surveillance at 'the boundaries of the precedented and at the limit of the thinkable'. Its conclusion, 'the unthinkable, after all, is that which covertly shapes our thoughts' may rank as a truism. But in so far as it offered some sort of useable purchase on a world of crumbling certainties, it is not to be blushed for.

In the circumstances, any subsequent, and surely final, effort can only modestly look back, marvelling that the series is still here, and not unreasonably congratulating itself on having provided an initial outlet for what turned, over the years, into some of the distinctive voices and topics in literary studies. But the volumes now re-presented have more than a mere historical interest. As their authors indicate, the issues they raised are still potent, the arguments with which they engaged are still disturbing. In short, we were not wrong. Academic study did change rapidly and radically to match, even to help to generate, wide-reaching social changes. A new set of discourses was developed to negotiate those upheavals. Nor has the process ceased. In our deliquescent world, what was unthinkable inside and outside the academy all those years ago now seems regularly to come to pass.

Whether the New Accents volumes provided adequate warning of, maps for, guides to, or nudges in the direction of this new terrain is scarcely for me to say. Perhaps our best achievement lay in cultivating the sense that it was there. The only justification for a reluctant third attempt at a Preface is the belief that it still is.

TERENCE HAWKES

ACKNOWLEDGEMENTS

The late Professor John D. Jump gave the idea of this book a good deal of encouragement at an early stage, for which I remain most grateful. I only wish its realization were more worthy of him.

I must thank Professor Victor Erlich of Yale University for generously making his specialized knowledge freely available to me, even as we swam in Cape Cod Bay. And I am particularly grateful to John Hartley of Queensland University of Technology for his tireless and scrupulous reading of some difficult passages, and for his invaluable corrective commentary upon them. The errors that remain are, needless to say, all my own work.

Any book whose mode is largely one of exposition and synthesis cannot fail to incur a wide-ranging obligation to other books. The present case is certainly no exception, and I have tried to ensure that the extent of that obligation is recognized for the most part in the pages that follow. However, I must also acknowledge a particular debt to three writers whose accounts of Structuralism have contributed decisively to the form and content of my own: Jonathan Culler, Fredric Jameson, Robert Scholes. I have drawn extensively upon their work and, although I have tried to indicate the measure of my debt to it in the normal manner in the text and bibliography, its influence throughout has proved pervasive and formative to a degree that has ultimately prohibited the detailed acknowledgement that is its due. I can only urge every reader of this book to become forthwith a reader of theirs.

I would also like to express my gratitude to the Trustees of the Leverhulme Foundation for their generous award of a research grant which proved especially helpful.

Finally, let me thank my own students at Cardiff, whose response to some of this material in an earlier form amply confirmed their capacity for the patient education of their teachers.

My greatest debt of gratitude remains what it has always been: to my wife.

T.H.

University College
  Cardiff

1

INTRODUCTION

To the average speaker of English, terms such as 'structure', 'structuralist' and 'structuralism' seem to have an abstract, complex, new-fangled and possibly French air about them: a condition traditionally offering uncontestable grounds for the profoundest mistrust.

But whatever the attractions of such anglo-saxon prejudices, they do not, on inspection, turn out to be particularly well-founded. The concept of 'structure', the notion of various 'structuralist' stances towards the world which might collectively be called 'structuralism', are not entirely alien to our trusted ways of thinking, nor did they spring, fully formed with horns and tail, out of the sulphurous Parisian atmosphere of the last decade.

VICO

In 1725 the distinguished Italian jurist Giambattista Vico published a book called *The New Science*. It was a momentous occasion, although it passed virtually unnoticed at the time. For the 'science' Vico proposed was nothing less than a science of human society. Its model was the 'natural' science of such men as Galileo, Bacon and Newton, and its aim was to perform for 'the world of nations' what these renaissance scientists had achieved for 'the world of nature'. Its goal, in short, was the construction of a 'physics of man'.

The master key of the new science lay in Vico's decisive perception that so-called 'primitive' man, when properly assessed, reveals himself not as childishly ignorant and barbaric, but as instinctively and characteristically 'poetic' in his response to the world, in that he possesses an inherent 'poetic wisdom' (*sapienza poetica*) which informs his responses to his environment and casts them in the form of a 'metaphysics' of metaphor, symbol and myth.

This 'discovery' – achieved only with the greatest difficulty because 'with our civilized natures we (moderns) cannot at all imagine and can understand only by great toil the poetic nature of these first men' (34)[1] – reveals that the apparently ludicrous and fanciful accounts of creation and the foundation of social institutions that occur in early societies, were not intended to be taken literally. They represent, not child-like 'primitive' responses to reality, but responses of quite a different order whose function was ultimately, and seriously, cognitive. That is, they embody, not 'lies' about the facts, but mature and sophisticated ways of knowing, of encoding, of presenting them. They constitute not mere embroidery of reality, but a way of coping with it: 'It follows that the first science to be learned should be mythology or the interpretation of fables; for, as we shall see, all the histories of the gentiles have their beginnings in fables' (51).

Myths, properly interpreted, can thus be seen to be 'civil histories of the first peoples who were everywhere naturally poets' (352). For example,

> The civil institutions in use under such kingdoms are narrated for us by poetic history in the numerous fables that deal with contests of song . . . and consequently refer to heroic contests over the auspices . . . Thus the satyr Marsyas . . . when overcome by Apollo in a contest of song, is flayed alive by the god . . . The sirens, who lull sailors to sleep with their song and then cut their throats; the Sphinx who puts

[1] The numbers refer to the passages of Vico's *The New Science* as given in the revised translation of the third edition, by Thomas Goddard Bergin and Max Harold Fisch, Ithaca and London: Cornell University Press, 1968.

riddles to travellers and slays them on their failure to find the solution; Circe, who by her enchantments turns into swine the comrades of Ulysses ... all these portray the politics of the heroic cities. The sailors, travellers, and wanderers of these fables are the aliens, that is, the plebeians who, contending with the heroes for a share in the auspices, are vanquished in the attempt and cruelly punished.

(646–8)

All myths, that is, have their grounding in the actual generalized experience of ancient peoples, and represent their attempts to impose a satisfactory, graspable, humanizing shape on it. That shape, argues Vico, springs from the human mind itself, and it becomes the shape of the world that that mind perceives as 'natural', 'given' or 'true'.

This establishes the principle of *verum factum*: that which man recognizes as true (*verum*) and that which he has himself made (*factum*) are one and the same. When man perceives the world, he perceives without knowing it the superimposed shape of his own mind, and entities can only be meaningful (or 'true') in so far as they find a place within that shape. So '. . . if we consider the matter well, poetic truth is metaphysical truth, and physical truth which is not in conformity with it should be considered false' (205).

In short, the 'physics of man' reveals that men have 'created themselves' (367), that 'the world of civil society has certainly been made by men, and that its principles are therefore to be found within the modifications of our own human mind' (331). Man seen thus is characteristically and pre-eminently a 'maker' (the Greek word for that being 'poet'), and the New Science will thus concentrate on a close study of the making or 'poeticizing' process.

This turns out to be a two-way affair of some complexity. For not only does man create societies and institutions in his own mind's image, but these in the end create him:

What Vico wanted to assert was that the first steps in the building of the 'world of nations' were taken by creatures who were still (or who had degenerated into) beasts, and that humanity itself was created by the very same processes by which institutions were created. Humanity is not a presupposition, but a consequence, an effect, a product of institution building.

(Bergin and Fisch, Introduction, op. cit. p. xliv)

That is, man constructs the myths, the social institutions, virtually the whole world as he perceives it, and in so doing he constructs himself. This making process involves the continual creation of recognizable and repeated forms which we can now term a process of *structuring*. Vico sees this process as an inherent, permanent and definitive human characteristic whose operation, particularly in respect of the creation of social institutions, is incessant and, because of its repetitive nature, predictable in its outcome.

> The nature of institutions is nothing but their coming into being at certain times and in certain guises. Whenever the time and guise are thus and so, such and not otherwise are the institutions that come into being (147).

Once 'structured' by man, the 'world of nations' proves itself to be a potent agency for continuous structuring: its customs and rites act as a forceful brainwashing mechanism whereby human beings are habituated to and made to acquiesce in a man-made world which they nevertheless perceive as artless and 'natural'.

Vico's work ranks as one of the first modern attempts to break the anaesthetic grip that such a permanent structuring process has on the human mind. It thus represents one of the first modern recognitions of that process as a definitive characteristic of that mind. *The New Science* links directly with those modern schools of thought whose first premise may be said to be that human beings and human societies are not fashioned after some model or plan which exists before they do. Like the existentialists, Vico seems to argue that there is no pre-existent, 'given' human essence, no predetermined 'human nature'. Like the Marxists, he seems to say that particular forms of humanity are determined by particular social relations and systems of human institutions.

The one genuinely distinctive and permanent human characteristic is discernible in the faculty of 'poetic wisdom', which manifests itself as the capacity and the necessity to generate myths, and to use language metaphorically: to deal with the world, that is, not directly but at one remove, by means of other agencies: not literally, but 'poetically'. 'There must', Vico insists, 'in the nature of human institutions be a mental language common to all nations which uniformly grasps the substance of things feasible in human social life and expresses it with as many diverse modifications as these same things may have diverse aspects' (161). This 'mental language' manifests itself as man's universal capacity not only to formulate structures, but also to submit his own nature to the demands of their structuring. The gift of *sapienza poetica* could thus be said to be the gift of structuralism. It is a principle which informs the way all human beings always live. To be human, it claims, is to be a structuralist.

PIAGET

If we are all structuralists, then we ought to know what a *structure* is. Yet that key concept can be uncomfortably elusive, and we ought now to try to move rather closer to it.

One of the most fruitful attempts at a definition has been made by Jean Piaget.[1] Structure, he argues, can be observed in an arrangement of entities which embodies the following fundamental ideas:

(a) the idea of wholeness
(b) the idea of transformation
(c) the idea of self-regulation

By *wholeness* is meant the sense of internal coherence. The arrangement of entities will be complete in itself and not something that is simply a composite formed of otherwise independent elements. Its constituent parts will conform to a set of intrinsic laws which determine its nature and theirs. These laws confer on the constituent parts within the structure overall properties larger than those each individually possesses outside it. Thus a *structure* is quite different from an *aggregate*: its constituent parts have no genuinely independent existence outside the structure in the same form that they have within it.

[1] Jean Piaget, *Structuralism*, pp. 5–16.

The structure is not static. The laws which govern it act so as to make it not only structured, but *structuring*. Thus, in order to avoid reduction to the level merely of passive form, the structure must be capable of *transformational* procedures, whereby new material is constantly processed by and through it. So language, a basic human structure, is capable of transforming various fundamental sentences into the widest variety of new utterances while retaining these within its own particular structure.

Finally, the structure is *self-regulating* in the sense that it makes no appeals beyond itself in order to validate its transformational procedures. The transformations act to maintain and underwrite the intrinsic laws which bring them about, and to 'seal off' the system from reference to other systems. A language, to take the previous example, does not construct its formations of words by reference to the patterns of 'reality', but on the basis of its own internal and self-sufficient rules. The word 'dog' exists, and functions within the structure of the English language, without reference to any four-legged barking creature's real existence. The word's behaviour derives from its inherent structural status as a noun rather than its referent's actual status as an animal. Structures are characteristically 'closed' in this way.

STRUCTURALISM

It follows that structuralism is fundamentally a way of thinking about the world which is predominantly concerned with the perception and description of structures, as defined above. As a developing concern of modern thinkers since Vico, it is the result of a momentous historic shift in the nature of perception which finally crystallized in the early twentieth century, particularly in the field of the physical sciences, but with a momentum that has carried through to most other fields. The 'new' perception involved the realization that despite appearances to the contrary the world does not consist of independently existing objects, whose concrete features can be perceived clearly and individually, and whose nature can be classified accordingly. In fact, every perceiver's *method* of perceiving can be shown to contain an inherent bias which affects what is perceived to a significant degree. A wholly objective perception of individual entities is therefore not possible: any observer is bound to *create* something of what he observes. Accordingly, the *relationship* between observer and observed achieves a kind of primacy. It becomes the only thing that *can* be observed. It becomes the stuff of reality itself. Moreover the principle involved must invest the whole of reality. In consequence, the true nature of things may be said to lie not in things themselves, but in the relationships which we construct, and then perceive, *between* them.

This new concept, that the world is made up of relationships rather than things, constitutes the first principle of that way of thinking which can properly be called 'structuralist'. At its simplest, it claims that the nature of every element in any given situation has no significance by itself, and in fact is determined by its relationship to all the other elements involved in that situation. In short, the full significance of any entity or experience cannot be perceived unless and until it is integrated into the *structure* of which it forms a part.

It follows that the ultimate quarry of structuralist thinking will be the permanent structures into which individual human acts, perceptions, stances fit, and from which they derive their final nature. This will finally involve what Fredric Jameson has described as 'an explicit search for the permanent structures of the mind itself, the organizational categories and forms through which the mind is able to experience the world, or to organize a meaning in what is essentially in itself meaningless'.[1] The ghost of Vico clearly remains unplaced.

Nevertheless, we must set our sights a little lower than the 'permanent structures of the mind' for the moment, and concentrate on the impact that the structuralist way of thinking has had on the study of literature. As we do so, we might remind ourselves that, of all the arts, that involving the use of words remains most closely related to that aspect of his nature which makes man distinctive: language. And it is not accidental that many of the concepts now central to structuralism were first fully developed in connection with the modern study of language: linguistics; and with the modern study of man: anthropology. Few spheres could be closer to the mind's 'permanent structures' than those.

---

[1] Fredric Jameson, *The Prison-House of Language: A Critical Account of Structuralism and Russian Formalism*, p. 109.

2

LINGUISTICS AND ANTHROPOLOGY

SAUSSURE

We can begin with the work of Ferdinand de Saussure, a Swiss linguist whose work forms the groundbase on which most contemporary structuralist thinking now rests. Saussure inherited the traditional view already referred to, that the world consists of independently existing objects, capable of precise objective observation and classification. In respect of linguistics this outlook yields a notion of language as an aggregate of separate units, called 'words', each of which somehow has a separate 'meaning' attached to it, the whole existing within a *diachronic* or historical dimension which makes it subject to observable and recordable laws of change.

Saussure's revolutionary contribution to the study of language lies in his rejection of that 'substantive' view of the subject in favour of a 'relational' one, a change of perspective closely in accord with the larger shift in perception mentioned above. It is recorded in his *Cours de Linguistique Générale*, the account, put together from notes taken by his students, of a series of lectures which he delivered at the University of Geneva between 1906 and 1911, and published posthumously in 1915. The *Cours* presents the argument that language should be studied, not only in terms of its individual parts, and not only diachronically, but also in terms of the relationship *between* those parts, and *synchronically*: that is, in terms of its *current* adequacy. In short, he proposed that a language should be studied as a *Gestalteinheit*, a unified 'field', a self-sufficient system, as we actually experience it *now*.

Saussure's insistence on the importance of the *synchronic* as distinct from the *diachronic* study of language was momentous because it involved recognition of language's current *structural* properties as well as its *historical* dimensions. As Fredric Jameson puts it 'Saussure's original-ity was to have insisted on the fact that language as a total system is complete at every moment, no matter what happens to have been altered in it a moment before.'[1] Each language, that is, has a wholly valid existence *apart* from its history, as a system of sounds issuing from the lips of those who speak it now, and whose speech in fact constructs and constitutes the language (usually in ignorance of its history) in its present form.

Saussure begins with a consideration of the whole phenomenon of language in terms of two fundamental dimensions which it exhibits: that of *langue* and that of *parole*. The dialectical distinction he draws between these two has proved of fundamental importance to the development of linguistics in general and of structuralism in particular.

The distinction between *langue* and *parole* is more or less that which pertains between the abstract language-system which in English we call simply 'language', and the individual utterances made by speakers of the language in concrete everyday situations which we call 'speech'. Saussure's own analogy is the distinction between the abstract set of rules and conventions called 'chess', and the actual concrete games of chess played by people in the real world. The rules of chess can be said to exist above and beyond each individual game, and yet they only ever acquire concrete form in the relationships that develop between the pieces in individual games. So with language. The nature of the *langue* lies beyond, and determines, the nature of each manifestation of *parole*, yet it has no concrete existence of its own, except in the piecemeal manifestations that speech affords.

Man can be described as the animal who characteristically devises

[1] Jameson, *op. cit.*, pp. 5–6.

and invests in language: that is, in a complex system or structure of correspondences between distinct signs, and distinct ideas or 'meanings' to which those signs distinctively relate. It happens – perhaps by accident – that the vocal apparatus has become the chief instrument and vehicle for language's concrete actualization in the real world of social intercourse. Nevertheless, '. . . what is natural to mankind is not oral speech but the faculty of constructing a language, i.e. a system of distinct signs corresponding to distinct ideas' (p. 10).[1] This faculty, termed 'the linguistic faculty proper' lies in fact 'beyond the functioning of the various organs', and may be thought of as 'a more general faculty which governs signs' (p. 11). And what that faculty or power to construct signs generates in respect of language may be thought of as the larger structure which, though we never see or hear it in actual physical terms, can be deduced from its momentary manifestation in actual human utterances. *Langue* is therefore 'both a social product of the faculty of speech and a collection of necessary conventions that have been adopted by a social body to permit individuals to exercise that faculty' (p. 9). *Parole*, it follows, is the small part of the iceberg that appears above the water. *Langue* is the larger mass that supports it, and is implied by it, both in speaker and hearer, but which never itself appears.

The fact that language is intangible and never appears all at once in its entirety, but only in the incomplete performance of part of the repertoire by individual speakers has, since Saussure, offered a fruitful direction in which modern linguistics might move. That is, towards a description of the full pattern of systematized relationships which individual utterances and understanding point at and presuppose: towards, to use the modified terminology proposed by more recent linguists such as Noam Chomsky, an account of the system of 'competence' that must precede, and that must (to use his terminology again) 'generate' individual 'performance'. Not surprisingly, where individual *performance*, or *parole* seems heterogeneous, without pattern, without systematic coherence, its preceding *competence*, or *langue* seems homogeneous. It exhibits, in short, a discernible structure.

[1] Page references are to the translation of Saussure's *Cours de Linguistique Générale* by Wade Baskin; *Course in General Linguistics*, New York, 1959.

The full implications of this turn out to be fundamentally chal-
lenging, in that they require us to relinquish what Charles C. Fries has
called an 'item-centered' view of the world, and the 'word-centred
thinking about language'[1] produced by it, in favour of the sort of
'relational' or 'structural' view already referred to. If no 'item' has any
significance by itself, but derives its significance entirely from its relationship with other items, then this must affect our thinking about
language at a very basic level. We can begin with the *sounds* made by the
human voice.

At this fundamental *phonetic* level, it quickly becomes clear that a large
number of different 'items' are indeed in operation, and we only have
to listen to an ordinary conversation to establish their range and complexity. Yet it is also clear that what makes any single item 'meaningful'
is not its own particular individual quality, but the *difference* between
this quality and that of other sounds. In fact, the differences are systematized into 'oppositions' which are linked in crucial relationships.
Thus, in English, the established *difference* between the initial sound of *tin*
and the initial sound of *kin* is what enables a different 'meaning' to be
given to each word. This is to say that the meaning of each word
resides in a structural sense in the difference between its own sounds
and those of other words. In this case, the English language has registered the contrast or sense of 'opposition' between the sound of /t/ in
tin and the sound of /k/ in *kin* as significant, that is, as capable of
generating meaning.

However, much more crucial is the fact that by no means every
possible contrast is registered as significant by the language. In fact,
large numbers of contrasts are ignored by it, and only a relatively small
proportion of the differences that actually occur between sounds are
recognized as different for the purpose of forming words and creating
meaning. Those that are not so recognized – however different they
may be in fact – are simply lumped together as 'the same'. For example,
the /p/ sound as it occurs in *pin* is obviously very different from what
we habitually term 'the same' /p/ sound as it appears in *spin*: and there
is a no less clear difference between the first consonant of *coal* and the
first consonant of *call*. No 'foreign' speaker of English would ever call

---

[1] Charles C. Fries, *Linguistics and Reading*, p. 64.

these sounds 'the same'. We do, simply because the differences between them are not 'recognized' in English, in the sense that they are never used to distribute 'meaning' between words.

What we encounter here is a fundamental *structuring* principle. It is one which characteristically overrides the 'actual' nature of individual items, and systematically imposes its own shape or pattern upon them. When we look closely at the process we can see that it works by forcing us (whether we like it or not) to distinguish between two kinds or levels of 'difference'. There is that which *actually* occurs (*coal/call*) on the *phonetic* level, but which the *structure* of the language does not register, and which its speakers accordingly do not, when they speak the language, recognize. And then there is that which also actually occurs, but which since the structure of the language *does* take account of it, is recognized. This 'recognized' level is called the *phonemic* level, the items which appear on it are called *phonemes*, and it is these sounds (as in the first consonants of *tin* and *kin*) that the speakers of the language hear as 'different', that is, as opposed in a pattern of meaningful contrasts. The point is that of the many 'samenesses' or differences that actually occur (or have diachronically occurred) in the language, we only perceive those which the language's *synchronic* structure makes meaningful, and vice versa.

The arrangement which makes them so could be called both arbitrary and systematic. 'Arbitrary' because it is self-contained and self-justifying: there is no appeal possible beyond it to some category of the 'natural' or the 'real' which would justify *tin/kin*'s 'difference' and deny that of *coal/call*. And 'systematic' because, by the same token, we feel ourselves to be in the presence (and in the grip) of a firmly rooted and overriding *system* of relationships governed by general laws which determine the status of each and every individual item it contains.

Such a system, encountered even at this primary level, can properly be termed *structural*. It is perceived as a *synchronic* phenomenon. And since it occurs at the very moment when language emerges as speech, the *phonemic principle* which animates it can be said to be a (if not the) fundamental structural concept. The notion of a complex pattern of paired functional differences, of 'binary opposition' as it has been termed, is clearly basic to it. In fact, the principle is common to all languages. As Roman Jakobson and Morris Halle point out, the discernment of binary opposition is a child's 'first logical operation', and in that operation we see the primary and distinctive intervention of culture into nature.[1] There are thus grounds for recognizing, in the capacity for the creation and perception of binary or paired 'opposites', and in the cognate activity of the creation and perception of phonemic patterning at large, a fundamental and characteristic operation of the human mind. It is an operation which creates structures.

But Saussure goes further. Language, after all, inheres not in 'the material substance of words' (p. 18) but in the larger and abstract 'system of signs' of which those words are the barest tip. In fact, 'signs and their relations are what linguistics studies' (p. 102) and the nature both of signs and of the relationship between them is also seen to be structural.

The linguistic sign can be characterized in terms of the relationship which pertains between its dual aspects of 'concept' and of 'sound-image' – or, to use the terms which Saussure's work has made famous – *signified* (*signifié*) and *signifier* (*signifiant*). The structural relationship between the concept of a tree (i.e. the *signified*) and the sound-image made by the word 'tree' (i.e. the *signifier*) thus constitutes a linguistic sign, and a language is made up of these: it is 'a system of signs that express ideas' (p. 16).

Since language is fundamentally an *auditory* system, the relationship between signifier and signified unfolds during a passage of time. Where a painting can display and juxtapose its elements at the same time, verbal utterance lacks that kind of simultaneity and is forced to deliver its elements in a certain order or sequence which is itself significant. In short, the mode of the relationship between signifier and signified can be said to be essentially, albeit minimally, sequential in nature.

The overall characteristic of this relationship is one that we have already encountered: it is arbitrary. There exists no necessary 'fitness' in the link between the sound-image, or signifier 'tree', the concept, or signified that it involves, and the actual physical tree growing in the earth. The word 'tree', in short, has no 'natural' or 'tree-like' qualities, and there is no appeal open to a 'reality' beyond the structure of the language in order to underwrite it.

---

[1] Roman Jakobson and Morris Halle, *Fundamentals of Language*, pp. 60–1.

The very arbitrariness of the linguistic sign protects it from change. As Saussure says 'any subject in order to be discussed must have a reasonable basis' (p. 73). But the arbitrariness of the linguistic sign is not 'reasonable', and so it cannot be discussed in the sense that we cannot profitably consider or debate its adequacy. The sign is simply there. There is literally no reason to prefer any other word from any other source, *arbre, baum, arbor* or even an invented word, *fnurd*, to 'tree'. None is more adequate or 'reasonable' than another. The word 'tree' means the physical leafy object growing in the earth because the *structure of the language* makes it mean that, and only validates it when it does so. It follows that language acts as a great *conservative* force in human apprehension of the world.

In fact, the very arbitrariness of the relationship between signifier and signified that makes language conservative in nature also serves to guarantee the 'structural' nature of the system in which it occurs in precisely the terms put forward by Piaget. Language is self-defining, and so whole and complete. It is capable of a process of 'transformation': that is, of generating new aspects of itself (new sentences) in response to new experience. It is self-regulating. It has these capacities precisely because it allows no single, unitary appeals to a 'reality' beyond itself. In the end, it constitutes its own reality.

In other words, language stands as the supreme example of a self-contained 'relational' structure whose constituent parts have no significance unless and until they are integrated within its bounds. As Saussure puts it, 'Language is a system of inter-dependent terms in which the value of each term results solely from the simultaneous presence of the others' (p. 114).

If all aspects of the language are thus 'based on relations' (p. 122) two dimensions of these relationships must assume particular importance. Saussure presents these as the linguistic sign's *syntagmatic* (or 'horizontal') relations, and its simultaneous *associative* (or 'vertical') relations.

It has been pointed out that the mode of language is fundamentally one of sequential movement through time. It follows from this that each word will have a linear or 'horizontal' relationship with the words that precede and succeed it, and a good deal of its capacity to 'mean' various things derives from this pattern of positioning. In the sentence 'the boy kicked the girl', the meaning 'unrolls' as each word follows its predecessor and is not complete until the final word comes into place. This constitutes language's syntagmatic aspect, and it could also be thought of as its 'diachronic' aspect because of its commitment to the passage of time.

But each word will also have relationships with other words in the language that do not occur at this point in time, but are *capable* of doing so. The word, that is, has 'formulaic' associations with those other words from among which it has, so to speak, been chosen. And these other words, 'part of the inner storehouse that makes up the language of each speaker' (p. 123) – they might be synonyms, antonyms, words of similar sound or of the same grammatical function – help, by *not* being chosen, to define the meaning of the word which has. It obviously follows from our notion of language as a self-contained structure that the *absence* of certain words partly creates and certainly winnows and refines the meanings of those that are present, and in the above sentence, part of the meaning of 'kicked' derives from the fact that it turns out *not* to be 'kissed' or 'killed' as the full relationships of the words in the sentence are unrolled. These kinds of relationships can be thought of as on a 'vertical' plane to distinguish them from the simultaneously operating yet quite distinct relationships of the horizontal, syntagmatic plane. They constitute the word's *associative* aspect, and obviously form part of its 'synchronic' relationship with the whole language structure (pp. 122–7).

Thus, the value of any linguistic 'item' is finally and wholly determined by its total environment: 'it is impossible to fix even the value of the word signifying "sun" without first considering its surroundings: in some languages it is not possible to say "sit in the *sun*" ' (p. 116).

Ultimately, it seems that the very *concepts* a language expresses are also defined and determined by its structure. They exist, not intrinsically, as themselves ('Hebrew does not recognize even the fundamental distinctions between the past, present and future. Proto-Germanic has no special form for the future' (pp. 116–17)) and not positively, by their actual content, but negatively, by their formal differentiating relations with the other terms in the structure. 'Their most precise characteristic is in being what the others are not' (p. 117).

In thus focusing attention on what might be called the distinctive 'oppositional' mode in which linguistic structures are cast, Saussure seems finally to reinforce their 'closed' self-sufficient, self-defining nature, and to make them look inwards, to their own mechanisms, not outwards to a 'real' world that lies beyond them. Signs, like phonemes, function 'not through their intrinsic value but through their relative position', and thus – since the total mode of language is oppositional – '. . . whatever distinguishes one sign from the others constitutes it.' As a result, 'in language there are only differences *without positive terms*. Whether we take the signified or the signifier, language has neither ideas nor sounds that existed before the linguistic system, but only conceptual and phonic differences that have issued from the system' (pp. 118–21).

Language seen thus must finally be judged to be 'a form and not a substance' (p. 122): it is a structure which has *modes*, rather than an aggregate of items which has *content*.

And since this self-regarding, self-regulating form constitutes our characteristic means of encountering and of coping with the world beyond ourselves, then perhaps we can say that it constitutes the characteristic human structure. From there, it is only a small step to the argument that perhaps it also constitutes the characteristic structure of human reality.

That step takes us across the Atlantic.

AMERICAN STRUCTURAL LINGUISTICS

We have noted that Saussure's *Cours de Linguistique Générale* was first delivered as a series of lectures in Geneva between 1906 and 1911. In the form of notes taken by students, the *Cours* was published posthumously in French in 1915. Although its ideas proved widely influential in Europe, the First World War broke down contacts between European linguists and those active in North America, the rift was widened by the Second World War, and an English translation of Saussure's *Cours* did not appear until 1959.

As a result of this, and also as a result of the existence to hand, as it were, of a large number of Indian languages unknown to European linguists, the study of language in North America became a separate and independently flourishing growth. In Saussure's terms, its main thrust was towards synchronic accounts of native Indian languages. These were often begun for the purposes of furthering religious missionary work, but an additional impetus came from a sense of urgency that many of these languages were fast disappearing. The necessity simply to record and analyse them took precedence over any concern with the construction of general linguistic theories to an extent that seemed to make the term 'descriptive linguistics' wholly appropriate as far as its early practitioners, such as Franz Boas (1858–1942), as well as its historians were concerned.

One of the most important and influential of the American 'descriptive' linguists after Boas was Edward Sapir (1884–1939) and it was his work which formed the basis of what in America came to be termed 'structural linguistics'. As Fries argues, Sapir's book *Language* (1921) marks a significant breakthrough, for in it he records his growing awareness that languages operate by means of some kind of inherent structuring principle which simply overrides the 'objective' observations and expectations of the non-native speaker, who listens from 'outside':

I found that it was difficult or impossible to teach an Indian to make phonetic distinctions that did not correspond to 'points in the pattern of his language' however these differences might strike our objective ear, but that subtle, barely audible phonetic differences, if only they hit the 'points in the pattern' were easily and voluntarily expressed in writing . . .

(*Language* p. 56n.)

In short, like Saussure, Sapir discovered that the *phonetic* difference between two sounds only becomes meaningful to the native speaker when it coincides with the *phonemic* structure (or 'points in the pattern') of the language in which it occurs. Moreover, that structure has a considerable 'anaesthetic' effect on the native speaker's perception of his own language. He finds it very difficult to hear distinctions that the phonemic structure does not 'recognize'.

By the time Leonard Bloomfield had published his enormously influential book *Language* (1933) linguistics in America had followed Sapir's insights to such a degree that it could be called 'structural' without falsification, although the term conventionally applied to this mode of linguistic analysis remained the looser one 'descriptive'. The climax of work in this vein, certainly in the field of phonology, is probably represented by the publication in 1951 of Trager and Smith's significantly titled *Outline of English Structure*.

Meanwhile, as a result of first hand contact with 'exotic' cultures that had been denied to European linguists, American structural linguistics – always closely linked with anthropology – had made progress in another area: that of the relationship between language and the cultural 'setting' in which it occurred. As the life of Indian tribesmen came more and more closely to be studied, this relationship seemed to have both a reflective and a formative character.

We have noticed that a language's structuring agency seems to exert an 'anaesthetic' power which makes it difficult for its speakers to register sounds that do not conform to the 'contrastive' or oppositional patterns of its phonemes. The same power makes it very difficult for us even to form or utter sounds used phonemically in other languages that do not fit the phonemic structure of our own. This is what gives foreign speakers their 'foreign' accents. The silent effectiveness of this power is such that it would therefore be surprising if each language's structure did not finally make its impress upon habits of perception and response that ultimately extend beyond itself. And indeed, when Sapir, and later the influential B. L. Whorf, made their initial extensions of linguistic structuring into other fields of social behaviour, they quickly reached the conclusion that the 'shape' of a culture, or total way of life of a community, was in fact determined by – or at any rate clearly 'structured' in the same way as – that culture's language. There is therefore, concluded Sapir in a classic statement, no such thing as an objective, unchanging 'real world':

> Human beings do not live in the objective world alone, nor alone in the world of social activity as ordinarily understood, but are very much at the mercy of the particular language which has become the medium of expression for their society. It is quite an illusion to imagine that one adjusts to reality essentially without the use of language and that language is merely an incidental means of solving specific problems of communication or reflection. The fact of the matter is that the 'real world' is to a large extent built up on the language habits of the group.

> No two languages are ever sufficiently similar to be considered as
> representing the same social reality. The worlds in which different
> societies live are distinct worlds, not merely the same world with dif-
> ferent labels attached ... We see and hear and otherwise experience
> very largely as we do because the language habits of our community
> predispose certain choices of interpretation.
>
> (*Selected Writings in Language, Culture and Personality*, p. 162)

The assumption fundamental to this conception is that the world of
space and time is in fact a continuum, without firm and irrevocable
boundaries or divisions, which each language divides up and encodes
in accordance with its own particular structure. As Dorothy Lee
expresses it,

> ... a member of a given society – who, of course, codifies experienced
> reality through the use of the specific language and other patterned
> behaviour characteristic of his culture – can actually grasp reality only
> as it is presented to him in this code. The assumption is not that
> reality itself is relative, but that it is differently punctuated and categor-
> ized by participants of different cultures, or that different aspects of it
> are noticed by, or presented to, them.[1]

In short, a culture comes to terms with nature by means of 'encoding',
through language. And it requires only a slight extension of this view
to produce the implication that perhaps the entire field of social
behaviour which constitutes the culture might in fact also represent an
act of 'encoding' on the model of language. In fact, it might itself *be* a
language.

CLAUDE LÉVI-STRAUSS

This, in essence, was the view taken by a number of anthropologists
whose work began to appear during and just after the Second World
War. Chief among them, and the one whose committed pursuit of the

---

[1] Dorothy Lee, 'Lineal and nonlineal codifications of reality' in Edmund Carpenter and
Marshall McLuhan (eds.) *Explorations in Communication*, Boston, 1960, pp. 136–54.

principles involved has most helped to attract the epithet 'structuralist' to his discipline, was the French anthropologist Claude Lévi-Strauss.

The notion of a myth-making 'poetic wisdom' which animates the response to the world of so-called 'primitive peoples' is a fundamental principle of Lévi-Strauss's thought. This of course links him directly with Vico, a connection confirmed by his ultimate aim to produce a 'general science of man' as well as by his basic conviction that 'men have *made* themselves to no less an extent than they have made the races of their domestic animals, the only difference being that the process has been less conscious or voluntary'.[1] The same concern also links him with the thinking of Marx and Lévi-Strauss has acknowledged that connection in his remark that 'the famous statement by Marx, "men make their own history, but they do not know that they are making it" justifies first, history, and second, anthropology' (*SA*, p. 23).

However, while he also shares Vico's interest in language as a major aspect of the 'science of man', he is to be distinguished both from the Italian jurist and the German philosopher by the extent of his concern to utilize the methods of modern linguistics in his analysis of nonlinguistic data: by his very American notion (directly derived, as he recognizes, from the work of Whorf, Sapir and others) that since language is man's overwhelmingly distinctive feature, it constitutes 'at once the prototype of the *cultural phenomenon* (distinguishing man from the animals) and the phenomenon whereby all the forms of social life are established and perpetuated (*SA*, pp. 358–9). As he put it in his famous book *Tristes Tropiques* (1955) 'Qui dit homme, dit langage, et qui dit langage dit société.'

The central question to emerge from such a viewpoint is the one raised above: in Lévi-Strauss's words, 'whether the different aspects of social life (including even art and religion) cannot only be studied by the methods of, and with the help of concepts similar to those employed in linguistics, but also whether they do not constitute phenomena whose inmost nature is the same as that of language' (*SA*, p. 62).

If that were indeed the case, then the analysis of language would

---

[1] 'Claude Lévi-Strauss, *Structural Anthropology* (Penguin Books, 1972), p. 353. I shall hereafter refer to this work as *SA*.

obviously suggest an appropriate model for the analysis of culture at large. And at one level, however manifold and complex his contribution to the broader fields of 'structuralism' might be, the general drift of Lévi-Strauss's work has ultimately been directed towards an investigation of the validity of that proposition.

Like the linguist, he sets out to identify the genuinely constitutive elements of what appears at first sight to be an apparently disparate and shapeless mass of phenomena. His method, fundamentally, involves the application to this non-linguistic material of the principles of what he himself terms the 'phonological revolution' brought about by the linguist's concept of the phoneme. That is, he attempts to perceive the constituents of cultural behaviour, ceremonies, rites, kinship relations, marriage laws, methods of cooking, totemic systems, not as intrinsic or discrete entities, but in terms of the contrastive relationships they have with each other that make their structures analogous to the phonemic structure of a language. Thus, 'like phonemes, kinship terms are elements of meaning; like phonemes, they acquire meaning only if they are integrated into systems' (SA, p. 34) and 'like language . . . the cuisine of a society may be analysed into constituent elements, which in this case we might call "gustemes", and which may be organized according to certain structures of opposition and correlation' (SA, p. 86).

To correct the error of Whorf, whose studies Lévi-Strauss sees as lacking an integrating theory, being merely empirical, atomistic, and concerned with the parts and not the whole of a culture (SA, p. 85), these systems should be seen to combine to form 'a kind of language, a set of processes, permitting the establishment between individuals and groups, of a certain type of communication' (SA, p. 61). Each system, that is, kinship, food, political ideology, marriage ritual, cooking, etc. constitutes a *partial* expression of the total culture, conceived ultimately as a single gigantic *language*. Moreover, '. . . if we find these structures to be common to several spheres, we have the right to conclude that we have reached a significant knowledge of the unconscious attitudes of the society or societies under consideration' (SA, p. 87).

Perhaps the best way of indicating the fruitful nature of this pursuit of 'unconscious attitudes' is to try to give an account of Lévi-Strauss's analysis of three specific 'systems' which seem to yield valuable material: those of kinship, myth, and the nature of the 'savage' mind.

Kinship

All societies have 'kinship' systems: that is, sets of 'rules' concerning who may – and more often who may not – marry whom and prescribing the nature of familial relationships at large. (A good example is the 'Table of Kindred and Affinity' in the Church of England's *Book of Common Prayer*.) Lévi-Strauss proposes that such systems, or 'structures', may be homologous with the structure of the language of the society involved in them on the grounds that 'different types of communication systems in the same societies – that is, kinship and language' may in effect be produced by 'identical unconscious structures' (*SA*, p. 62). In any event, following the fundamental structuralist (and 'phonemic') principle that the relationship *between* phenomena determines their nature, not any intrinsic aspect of the phenomena themselves, Lévi-Strauss is able to look at the broader implications of kinship relationships in a new light. For instance, his view of the function of the exchange of women, or of the role of uncles (the *avunculate*) in primitive societies seems at once more profound and informative than that available to more 'empirical' observers.

> According to Radcliffe-Brown, the term *avunculate* covers two antithetical systems of attitudes. In one case, the maternal uncle represents family authority; he is feared and obeyed, and possesses certain rights over his nephew. In the other case, the nephew holds privileges of familiarity in relation to his uncle and can treat him more or less as his victim. Second, there is a correlation between the boy's attitude towards his maternal uncle and his attitude towards his father. We find the two systems of attitudes in both cases, but they are inversely correlated. In groups where familiarity characterizes the relationship between father and son, the relationship between maternal uncle and nephew is one of respect; and where the father stands as the austere representative of family authority, it is the uncle who is treated with familiarity.
>
> (*SA*, pp. 40–1)

By realizing that the two sets of attitudes involved here 'constitute (as the structural linguist would say) two pairs of oppositions' Lévi-Strauss is able to offer a radical modification of Radcliffe-Brown's view which, he argues, 'arbitrarily isolates particular elements of a global structure which must be treated as a whole'. Going beyond the limits of the 'empirical' scheme, and thus treating the whole structure involved, he ultimately discerns, to his own satisfaction at least, a general law:

> When we consider societies of the Cherkess and Trobriand types it is not enough to study the correlation of attitudes between *father/son* and *uncle/sister's son*. This correlation is only one aspect of a global system containing four types of relationships which are organically linked, namely: *brother/sister*, *husband/wife*, *father/son*, and *mother's brother/sister's son*. The two groups in our example illustrate a law which can be formulated as follows: In both groups, the relation between maternal uncle and nephew is to the relation between brother and sister as the relation between father and son is to that between husband and wife. Thus if we know one pair of relations, it is always possible to infer the other.
>
> (*SA*, p. 42)

Finally it becomes clear, after a lengthy analysis, that the avunculate system itself is structurally determined:

> Thus we see that in order to understand the avunculate we must treat it as one relationship within a system, while the system itself must be considered as a whole in order to grasp its structure. This structure rests upon four terms (brother, sister, father, and son), which are linked by two pairs of correlative oppositions in such a way that in each of the two generations there is always a positive relationship and a negative one. Now, what is the nature of this structure, and what is its function? The answer is as follows: This structure is the most elementary form of kinship that can exist. It is, properly speaking, *the unit of kinship*.
>
> (*SA*, p. 46)

The 'primitive and irreducible character' of this basic unit turns out on scrutiny to be 'actually a direct result of the universal presence of an incest taboo' since, in human society, 'a man must obtain a woman from another man, who gives him a daughter or a sister'. Hence, the presence of the maternal uncle in certain kinship structures is 'given' and, a fact which is invisible to mere empirical observation, functions as 'a necessary precondition for the structure to exist' (*SA*, p. 46).

Thus, if the biological family (which always exists) represents the gross 'phonetic' data of the kinship system, Lévi-Strauss feels that his own work enables him to describe items within it which have 'phonemic' status:

> ... we have interpreted the avunculate as a characteristic trait of elementary structure. This elementary structure, which is the product of defined relations involving four terms, is, in our view, the true *atom of kinship*. Nothing can be conceived or given beyond the fundamental requirements of its structure, and, in addition, it is the sole building block of more complex systems.
>
> (*SA*, p. 48)

In so far as traditional anthropological studies were unable to reach such conclusions, Lévi-Strauss feels justified in claiming that in this as in other respects, 'the error of traditional anthropology, like that of traditional linguistics, was to consider the terms and not the relations between the terms' (*SA*, p. 46). In this sense, the anthropologist deals, not in the 'objectively' observed facts of 'nature' but in those structures which the human mind characteristically superimposes on it:

> Of course, the biological family is ubiquitous in human society. But what confers upon kinship its socio-cultural character is not what it retains from nature, but, rather, the essential way in which it diverges from nature. A kinship system does not consist in the objective ties of descent or consanguinity between individuals. It exists only in human consciousness; it is an arbitrary system of representations, not the spontaneous development of a real situation.
>
> (*SA*, p. 50)

The social function of such a system is itself 'structural':

> ... kinship systems, marriage rules, and descent groups constitute a co-ordinated whole, the function of which is to insure the permanency

of the social group by means of intertwining consanguineous and affinal ties. They may be considered as the blueprint of a mechanism which 'pumps' women out of their consanguineous families to redistribute them in affinal groups, the result of this process being to create new consanguineous groups, and so on.

(*SA*, p. 309)

From this kind of emphasis on its 'arbitrary' and its 'systematic' character, the kinship system emerges clearly as 'a language' (*SA*, p. 47) – a structured and structuring system of signs, whose mode is symbolic, self-regulating and self-sufficient, requiring no reference to a 'reality' or 'nature' beyond itself to justify or validate its procedures:

Because they are symbolic systems, kinship systems offer the anthropologist a rich field, where his efforts can almost (and we emphasize the 'almost') converge with those of the most highly developed of the social sciences, namely, linguistics. But to achieve this convergence, from which it is hoped a better understanding of man will result, we must never lose sight of the fact that, in both anthropological and linguistic research, we are dealing strictly with symbolism. And although it may be legitimate or even inevitable to fall back upon a naturalistic interpretation in order to understand the emergence of symbolic thinking, once the latter is given, the nature of the explanation must change as radically as the newly appeared phenomenon differs from those which have preceded and prepared it. Hence, any concession to naturalism might jeopardize the immense progress already made in linguistics, which is also beginning to characterize the study of family structure, and might drive the sociology of the family toward a sterile empiricism, devoid of inspiration.

(*SA*, p. 51)

Myth

Of course, language itself remains the 'semantic system *par excellence*: it cannot but signify, and exists only through signification' (*SA*, p. 48). Nevertheless, from this sort of analysis it is quickly apparent that, like linguistics, anthropology is not concerned with the 'surface' of social life as consciously experienced by the member of the community, any more than the linguist is really concerned with the native speaker's often misleading conscious notions about the way his own language works. Mere empiricism is not enough. Mere 'naturalism' is misleading. In fact, the anthropologist's concern lies with the 'unconscious foundations' (*SA*, p. 18) on which that social life – and that language – rest. His quarry, in short, is the *langue* of the whole culture; its system and its general laws: he stalks it through the particular varieties of its *parole*.

The efficacy of these 'unconscious foundations' can be seen when they are tapped in such events as the shaman's (medicine man's) 'curing' of the sick in so-called primitive communities. As Lévi-Strauss points out, where modern science encourages us to see a causal relationship between germs and disease, the shaman's 'cure' rests upon his ability to relate the disease to the world of myth and monsters in which the sick person genuinely believes:

> That the mythology of the shaman does not correspond to an objective reality does not matter. The sick woman believes in the myth and belongs to a society which believes in it. The tutelary spirits and malevolent spirits, the supernatural monsters and magical animals, are all part of a coherent system on which the native conception of the universe is founded. The sick woman accepts these mythical beings or, more accurately, she has never questioned their existence. What she does not accept are the incoherent and arbitrary pains, which are an alien element in her system but which the shaman, calling upon myth, will re-integrate within a whole where everything is meaningful.
>
> Once the sick woman understands, however, she does more than resign herself; she gets well.
>
> (*SA*, p. 197)

In effect, what happens is that

> The shaman provides the sick woman with a *language*, by means of which unexpressed, and otherwise inexpressible, psychic states can be immediately expressed. And it is the transition to this verbal expression – at the same time making it possible to undergo in an ordered

and intelligible form a real experience that would otherwise be chaotic and inexpressible – which induces the release of the physiological process, that is, the reorganization, in a favourable direction, of the process to which the sick woman is subjected.

(Ibid., p. 198)

The relationship between language and myth thus occupies a central position in Lévi-Strauss's view of the 'savage' mind, and he argues that the nature of that mind reveals itself in the structures of its myths as much as in the structure of its language.

In the past, he points out, myths have been subjected to methods of interpretation which seriously conflict, not only with each other, but with the essential nature of the myths themselves. They have been seen as collective 'dreams', as the basis of ritual, as the result of 'a kind of esthetic play', and mythological figures themselves have been thought of as 'personified abstractions, divinized heroes, or fallen gods' (*SA*, p. 207). None of this can be considered satisfactory since it serves merely to reduce mythology to the level of childlike 'play', and denies it any more sophisticated relationship with the world, and with the society that generates it.

Lévi-Strauss's concern is ultimately with the extent to which the structures of myths prove actually formative as well as reflective of men's minds: the degree to which they dissolve the distinction between nature and culture. And so his aim, he says, is not to show how men think in myths, but 'how myths think in men, unbeknown to them'.[1] As in the case of kinship, the 'unconscious' structure of myth turns out to yield itself most readily to a 'phonemic' analysis of its phenomena, whereby the fantastic profusion of myths in the world may be reduced to a manageable number of recurrent elements, whose presence has genuine structural and structuring significance:

Whether the myth is recreated by the individual or borrowed from tradition, it derives from its sources – individual or collective ... – only the stock of representations with which it operates. But the

[1] 'Les mythes se pensent dans les hommes, et à leur insu'. Lévi-Strauss, *Le Cru et le Cuit*, p. 20.

> structure remains the same, and through it the symbolic function is fulfilled ... There are many languages, but very few structural laws which are valid for all languages. A compilation of known tales and myths would fill an imposing number of volumes. But they can be reduced to a small number of simple types if we abstract from among the diversity of characters a few elementary functions.
>
> (SA, pp. 203–4)

But as we pursue that small number of 'elementary functions', and seek to determine the nature of those structures which derive from them, mythology confronts us with a central problem:

> On the one hand it would seem that in the course of a myth anything is likely to happen. There is no logic, no continuity. Any characteristic can be attributed to any subject; every conceivable relation can be found. With myth, everything becomes possible. But on the other hand, this apparent arbitrariness is belied by the astounding similarity between myths collected in widely different regions ... If the content of a myth is contingent, how are we going to explain the fact that myths throughout the world are so similar?
>
> (SA, p. 208)

We can begin with the fundamental proposition mentioned above, that myth has obvious connections with language itself: 'to be known, myth has to be told: it is a part of human speech' (SA, p. 209) and so the analysis of it can properly aim to be 'the extension, to another field, of structural linguistics' (SA, p. 233).

Of course, the analogy is not exact and myth cannot be simply treated as language, for 'in order to preserve its specificity we must be able to show that it is both the same thing as language and also something different from it'. This 'sameness and difference' in fact is partly provided for in Saussure's fruitful distinction between *langue* and *parole*, structure and individual event. Myth obviously embodies this distinction in that the individual version of each myth, its *parole*, derives from and contributes to the fundamental structure of its *langue*: Sophocles's *Oedipus Rex* derives, as *parole*, from the *langue* of the total Oedipus myth. However, a third level is also discernible. A myth is always, in its individual telling, located in time: it always refers to events alleged to have happened a long time ago. Yet, in operation, the specific *pattern* or structure of events described is bound to be timeless; embracing, and linking in an explanatory mode the present with both past and future, while it is told. Thus, each time the myth is recounted, it combines both the elements of *langue* and *parole*, and in so doing transcends both, being, as an 'explanation' of the world, trans-historical and trans-cultural. This has its effect on the language involved. For the power of the *original* myth can never be affected by the way in which any particular version of it is recounted. Unlike poetry, myth does not suffer by 'translation': the poorest linguistic rendition of the events in the story is adequate to transmit the 'mythical value' of the myth. And so the language used in myth presents us with a peculiar sense of the existence of another meaningful level of operation beyond, or perhaps behind, the purely linguistic one:

> Whatever our ignorance of the language and the culture of the people where it originated, a myth is still felt as a myth by any reader anywhere in the world. Its substance does not lie in its style, its original music, or its syntax, but in the *story* which it tells. Myth is language, functioning on an especially high level where meaning succeeds practically at 'taking off' from the linguistic ground on which it keeps on rolling.
>
> (*SA*, p. 210)

Moreover, the 'correspondence' between a myth's 'meaning' and its 'content' can also be of a complex linguistic order:

> There must be, and there is, a correspondence between the unconscious meaning of a myth – the probem it tries to solve – and the conscious content it makes use of to reach that end, i.e. the plot. However, this correspondence should not always be conceived as a kind of mirror-image, it can also appear as a *transformation*.
>
> ('Four Winnebago Myths' in Richard and Fernande de George (eds.), *The Structuralists*, p. 201.)

Given this, Lévi-Strauss feels able to formulate two fundamental propositions in respect of myth:

1. The 'meaning' of mythology cannot reside in the isolated elements which constitute the myth, but must inhere in the way in which those elements are combined, and must take account of the potential for transformation that such a combination involves.

2. Language in myth exhibits specific properties, above the ordinary linguistic level (*SA*, p. 210).

From these it follows, first, that myth, like the rest of language, is made up of constituent units, and second, that these units presuppose and will be analogous to the constituent units discernible in ordinary language, in the form of phonemes, morphemes, etc. but will differ from these in that they also 'belong to a higher and more complex order' which entitles them to be called 'gross constituent units' or 'mythemes'. By breaking down a large number of myths into the smallest possible 'units' in the unfolding of its story, Lévi-Strauss discovers that although each unit consists of a 'relation' in which a certain function is linked to a given subject (e.g. 'Oedipus kills his father'), the true 'constituent units' of a myth 'are not the isolated relations themselves but *bundles of such relations*, and it is only as bundles that these relations can be put to use and combined so as to produce a meaning' (*SA*, p. 211). In short, like the phoneme in language, the 'bundle' is a set of items sharing the same functional trait. That the true 'mytheme' is a 'bundle' of this sort is the source of the curious effects already noticed in respect of myth: that however the myth is told, we sense, behind the individual telling or *parole*, and behind the *langue* from which that *parole* derives, a kind of *super-langue*, which emits a fundamental message. Of course, the message is in 'code', and the 'bundle' shows the code in operation.

A 'bundle' can best be defined as all the versions of a particular 'relation' that have ever existed, being simultaneously perceived, or sensed beneath and through whichever particular version is being used at any particular time. The 'bundles' function like phonemes, and their effect 'is as though a phoneme were always made up of all its variants' (*SA*, p. 212).

What Lévi-Strauss is trying to capture here is the sense of interaction between synchronic and diachronic dimensions, and between *langue* and *parole* that the telling of, say, the Oedipus myth will always generate:

the sense, that is, that we are always in the presence of a totally realizable potential; something that is *more* than a story being told here and now. A myth truly always consists 'of all its versions' (*SA*, p. 217). He is suggesting, in one sense, that myth always works simultaneously on two axes, rather as an orchestral score does, to achieve chording and harmony:

> an orchestra score, to be meaningful, must be read diachronically along one axis – that is, page after page, and from left to right – and synchronically along the other axis, all the notes written vertically making up one gross constituent unit, that is, one bundle of relations.
>
> (*SA*, p. 212)

Of course, when we hear any myth being told, we only ever encounter the 'orchestra score' line by line, diachronically, and we infer (or 'hear') the resonances of each 'bundle' as we go along, just as, to take another musical analogy, when we listen to a soloist in a jazz group we (and he) infer from his solo performance the original sequence of chords; the 'tune' from which it derives, and on which it contributes a tonal commentary.

To illustrate his argument, Lévi-Strauss presents his controversial 'decoding' of the 'score' of the Oedipus myth. It is worth quoting in full:

> The myth will be treated as an orchestra score would be if it were unwittingly considered as a unilinear series; our task is to re-establish the correct arrangement. Say, for instance, we were confronted with a sequence of the type: 1, 2, 4, 7, 8, 2, 3, 4, 6, 8, 1, 4, 5, 7, 8, 1, 2, 5, 7, 3, 4, 5, 6, 8 . . ., the assignment being to put all the 1's together, all the 2's, the 3's, etc.; the result is a chart:

$$
\begin{array}{ccccccc}
1 & 2 & & 4 & & & 7 & 8 \\
& & 2 & 3 & 4 & & 6 & 8 \\
1 & & & & 4 & 5 & & 7 & 8 \\
1 & 2 & & & & 5 & & 7 \\
& & & 3 & 4 & 5 & 6 & & 8
\end{array}
$$

> We shall attempt to perform the same kind of operation on the

Oedipus myth, trying out several arrangements of the mythemes until we find one which is in harmony with the principles enumerated above. Let us suppose, for the sake of argument, that the best arrangement is the following (although it might certainly be improved with the help of a specialist in Greek mythology):

Cadmos seeks his sister Europa, ravished by Zeus			
		Cadmos kills the dragon	
	The Spartoi kill one another		
			Labdacos (Laios' father) = *lame* (?)
	Oedipus kills his father, Laios		Laios (Oedipus' father) = *left-sided* (?)
		Oedipus kills the Sphinx	
			Oedipus = *swollen-foot* (?)
Oedipus marries his mother, Jocasta			
	Eteocles kills his brother, Polynices		
Antigone buries her brother, Polynices, despite prohibition			

We thus find ourselves confronted with four vertical columns, each of which includes several relations belonging to the same bundle. Were we to *tell* the myth, we would disregard the columns and read the rows from left to right and from top to bottom. But if we want to *understand* the myth, then we will have to disregard one half of the diachronic dimension (top to bottom) and read from left to right, column after column, each one being considered as a unit.

(*SA*, pp. 213–14)

It will be noticed that we are not concerned here to state the 'true' or the 'authentic' or the 'earliest' version of the myth. That is a mistaken quest, for if we genuinely define the myth as 'consisting of all its versions' it will remain 'the same' as long as it is 'fit' to do so (*SA*, p. 217). We are concerned in fact with the *langue* of the myth that lies behind all its *paroles*. Lévi-Strauss's 'reading' of the above 'mythemic' structure is highly contentious, but it may reassure us to notice that it is wholly in accord with Saussure's insistence on language's 'dual' aspect (associative or 'vertical' and syntagmatic or 'horizontal') as well as, we shall see later, with Jakobson's recognition of language's 'metaphoric' and 'metonymic' dimensions:

All the relations belonging to the same column exhibit one common feature which it is our task to discover. For instance, all the events grouped in the first column on the left have something to do with blood relations which are over-emphasized, that is, are more intimate than they should be. Let us say, then, that the first column has as its common feature the *overrating of blood relations*. It is obvious that the second column expresses the same thing, but inverted: *underrating of blood relations*. The third column refers to monsters being slain. As to the fourth, a few words of clarification are needed. The remarkable connotation of the surnames in Oedipus' father-line has often been noticed. However, linguists usually disregard it, since to them the only way to define the meaning of a term is to investigate all the contexts in which it appears, and personal names, precisely because they are used as such, are not accompanied by any context. With the method we propose to follow the objection disappears, since the myth itself provides its own context. The significance is no longer to be sought in the eventual meaning of each name, but in the fact that all the names have a common feature: All the hypothetical meanings (which may well remain hypothetical) refer to *difficulties in walking straight and standing upright*.

(*SA*, p. 215)

Accordingly, his conclusion as to the 'fundamental meaning' of the Oedipus myth is quintessentially 'structural' in mode:

The myth has to do with the inability, for a culture which holds the belief that mankind is autochthonous (see, for instance, Pausanias VIII, xxix, 4: plants provide a *model* for humans), to find a satisfactory transition between this theory and the knowledge that human beings are actually born from the union of man and woman. Although the problem obviously cannot be solved, the Oedipus myth provides a kind of logical tool which relates the original problem – born from one or born from two? – to the derivative problem: born from different or born from the same? By a correlation of this type, the overrating of blood relations is to the underrating of blood relations as the attempt to escape autochthony is to the impossibility to succeed in it. Although experience contradicts theory, social life validates cosmology by its similarity of structure. Hence cosmology is true.

(*SA*, p. 216)

This means, I take it, that Lévi-Strauss believes he has arrived at a method of analysis which furnishes 'rules of transformation' enabling us to shift from one variant of the myth to another. In the process, a mediating, validating, 'true-making' agency can be seen to operate which overcomes 'brute' reality and transforms it into its own image. Myth emerges as the 'logical tool' essential to this operation: one whereby we, in society, 'make up' reality as we go along, resolve what are in fact unresolvable 'oppositions', and so make our experiences adequate to our theoretical presuppositions: 'mythical thought always progresses from the awareness of oppositions toward their resolution' (*SA*, p. 224).

As a result, it is clear that analysis of this kind will quickly find itself reaching to the level of those unconscious categories of thought which underpin and formulate our total view of the world. The 'logic' of mythical thought, which derives from those categories, will obviously not seem particularly closely related to what we think of as 'ordinary' (that is, Aristotelian) scientifically inclined logic. But, as Lévi-Strauss concludes, 'the kind of logic in mythical thought is as rigorous as that of modern science and . . . the difference lies, not in the quality of the intellectual process, but in the nature of the things to which it is applied' (SA, p. 230). Man 'has always been thinking equally well' and his mind does not 'progress' so much as discover new areas to which its 'unchanged and unchanging powers' may be applied (SA, p. 230).

The 'savage' mind

When these conclusions are applied to so-called 'primitive' societies, they obviously acquire disturbing implications for our own. We are accustomed to think of such societies in negative terms:

> Anthropology, we are apt to say . . . is concerned with societies that are *non*-civilized, *without* a system of writing, and *pre*- or *non*-industrial in type. Yet behind all these qualifying negative expressions there is a positive reality. These societies are, to a far greater degree than others, based on personal relationships, on concrete relations between individuals . . .

> . . . In this respect it is, rather, modern societies that should be defined in negative terms. Our relations with one another are now only occasionally and fragmentarily based upon global experience, the concrete 'apprehension' of one person by another. They are largely the result of a process of indirect reconstruction, through written documents. We are no longer linked to our past by an oral tradition which implies direct contact with others (storytellers, priests, wise men or elders), but by books amassed in libraries, books from which we endeavour – with extreme difficulty – to form a picture of their authors. And we communicate with the immense majority of our contemporaries by all kinds of intermediaries – written documents or administrative machinery – which undoubtedly vastly extend our

contacts but at the same time make those contacts somewhat 'unauthentic'. This has become typical of the relationship between the citizen and the public authorities.

We should like to avoid describing negatively the tremendous revolution brought about by the invention of writing. But it is essential to realize that writing, while it conferred vast benefits on humanity, did in fact deprive it of something fundamental.

(*SA*, pp. 365–6)

The impact of writing (and of reading) on the human response to the world is clearly a matter of considerable interest to the student of literature, and its implications will be taken up at some length later in this book, when we consider the work of some of the 'structuralist' literary critics. For the moment, it will be sufficient to note that the 'fundamental' something that writing deprives us of is graphically described by Lévi-Strauss in his work on the nature of the so-called 'primitive' or 'savage' mind. In one sense that something inheres in the capacity of a man to invent *totems*: that is, to conceive of himself and his social system, quite sanely, in terms of other species: to say, in short, and with conviction, 'I am a bear', without thereby indicating his total lack of what earlier anthropologists have narrowly thought of as 'logic'. In fact, that 'something' could be said to be the capacity for a different kind of logic: a distinctive capacity to whose activities Lévi-Strauss gives the name *bricolage*.

The term *bricolage* is defined in his two major works on the primitive mind; *Totemism* (1962) and *The Savage Mind* (1962). It refers to the means by which the non-literate, non-technical mind of so-called 'primitive' man responds to the world around him. The process involves a 'science of the concrete' (as opposed to our 'civilized' science of the 'abstract') which, far from lacking logic, in fact carefully and precisely orders, classifies and arranges into structures the *minutiae* of the physical world in all their profusion by means of a 'logic' which is not our own. The structures, 'improvised' or 'made-up' (these are rough translations of the process of *bricoler*) as *ad hoc* responses to an environment, then serve to establish homologies and analogies between the ordering of nature and that of society, and so satisfactorily 'explain' the world and make it able to be lived in. The *bricoleur* constructs the totemic 'messages' whereby 'nature' and 'culture' are caused to mirror each other.[1]

A significant feature of *bricolage* is clearly the ease with which it enables the non-civilized, non-literate *bricoleur* to establish satisfactory analogical relationships between his own life and the life of nature instantaneously and without puzzlement or hesitation. His 'totemic' logic is not only structured, but structuring: its use of myth enables it to move effortlessly from one conceptual level to another:

> The mythical system and the modes of representation it employs serve to establish homologies between natural and social conditions or, more accurately, it makes it possible to equate significant contrasts found on different planes: the geographical, meteorological, zoo-logical, botanical, technical, economic, social, ritual, religious and philosophical.[2]

As a result, the 'savage', or better, the 'multi-conscious' mind, able and willing to respond to an environment on more than one level simul-taneously, and constructing in the process an elaborate and to us a bewilderingly complex 'world picture',

> builds mental structures which facilitate an understanding of the world in as much as they resemble it. In this sense savage thought can be defined as analogical thought.
>
> (SM, p. 263)

What is involved here is a 'reciprocity of perspectives' in which man and the world mirror each other by means of 'classificatory systems' which operate as 'systems of meaning' (SM, pp. 222–3). 'Analogical thought' works by imposing on the world a series of structural 'con-trasts' or 'oppositions' to which all the members of the culture tacitly assent and then proposing that these oppositions are analogically

[1] I have made the same point, with particular reference to the process of *bricolage* and the work of Lévi-Strauss, in *Metaphor* (London: Methuen, 1972), pp. 83–4. There the material forms part of a larger argument (pp. 78 ff.) concerning the relationship of language to reality.

[2] Lévi-Strauss, *The Savage Mind*, p. 93. I shall hereafter refer to this work as SM.

related in that their differences are felt to resemble each other. As a result an analysis of the analogical relationship between the oppositions of 'up' and 'down', 'hot' and 'cold', 'raw' and 'cooked' will offer insights into the nature of the particular 'reality' that each culture perceives.

A good example is the opposition between 'edible' and 'inedible' which all cultures maintain. Obviously the nature of the items placed under either of these two headings will crucially determine the way of life involved, since what is at stake is assent to the same 'ordering' of almost the entire natural world. 'Analogical thought' will move a culture to distinguish a 'foreign' culture from itself on this basis, so that the opposition 'edible–inedible' will become analogically related to the opposition 'native–foreign'. This means that 'transformations' between the two sets of 'similar differences' become possible: 'that which is inedible' becomes a metaphor of 'that which is foreign'. So, one of the persistent English metaphors for the French occurs because frogs' legs, placed under the heading 'edible' in France, find themselves under the heading 'inedible' in Britain. Moreover, the conventions which govern the cooking of food at large, the types of foods that may be combined and the kinds of food that may be eaten on various occasions turn out to be complex, coded sets of relationships relative to each individual culture, important as a major mediating factor between that culture and the nature that confronts it, and obviously maintaining a patterned set of analogies between other kinds of social relationships.

'Concrete' logic of this kind will, in its 'totemic' mode, see no difficulty in postulating 'a logical equivalence between a society of natural species and a world of social groups' (SM, p. 104). A man may think of himself as a bear because the analogy this evokes 'is not between social groups and natural species, but between the differences which manifest themselves on the level of groups on the one hand and on that of species on the other' (SM, p. 115). To say that clan A is 'descended' from the bear, and clan B from the eagle 'is nothing more than a concrete and abbreviated way of stating the relationship between A and B as analogous to a relationship between species'.[1] In other

---

[1] Lévi-Strauss, *Totemism*, trans. Rodney Needham, with an Introduction by Roger C. Poole, p. 100.

words, the man does not believe he is a bear, but the bear indicates his standing and role in the community, analogously defined, as part of a pattern of 'oppositions', against the standing of someone else. It represents just the sort of structure that we have seen, with Saussure, to be characteristic of language: a homology between two 'systems of differences' (*Totemism*, p. 150). And it once again underlines the structuralist insistence that the 'phonemic' relationship *between* entities is of more importance than the entities themselves, and indeed ultimately determines their nature. Thus the totemic 'code' acts as a 'linguistic' means of communication in the culture at large: it functions, as Roger C. Poole puts it, as a mode of 'discourse', a way of getting 'certain things said' (*Totemism*, p. 38). So, if we can accept Lévi-Strauss's argument that

> . . . the operative value of the systems of naming and classifying commonly called totemic derives from their formal character: they are codes suitable for conveying messages which can be transposed into other codes, and for expressing messages received by means of different codes in terms of their own system.
>
> (*SM*, pp. 75–6)

– we can also accept Poole's conclusion that '. . . the identification "I am a bear", which seemed to anthropologists of an earlier period to outrage the most sacred canons of logic' can now in fact be seen as 'a statement about the world, and about the individual's place in it, in relation to all other things and individuals in the world' (*Totemism*, p. 61). In other words, the statement 'I am a bear' is not illogical: it demonstrates the limits of our own particular kind of logic. It is a logic which lacks the conceptual tool by whose means the world can be encountered, not *as* another creature but, in a phrase whose implication clearly confirms the active presence of a code, 'by means of' that creature (*SM*, p. 149).

Anthropology is traditionally distinguished from history as the study of societies which have no written documents (*SA*, pp. 24–5). But so deeply does anthropology of the kind propounded by Lévi-Strauss probe into the 'encoding' or structuring capacity of the human mind, that one of its conclusions must be that it has encountered the essential nature of that mind in its fundamental form, regardless of the particular society in which it appears. It is a form which does not significantly vary in the case of the 'modern' technological mind however much that tends, misleadingly, to think of language, that formative, 'unreflecting totalization' of our experience, solely in its written mode. That mind, which exists in us no less than in 'primitive' man, proves to be a fundamentally 'structuring' agency of considerable power. And it is worth pondering the evident fact that one of the foremost manifestations of its structuring capacity, totemism, is not simply something in which 'savages' engage. In British sporting circles, a man may, however lamely, be called a 'Lion', a 'Springbok', a 'Wallaby' by means of a structured 'oppositional' system in respect of international rugby football, which involves the use of animal characteristics related to so-called 'national' temperaments. And as Edmund Leach points out

> It is a fact of empirical observation that human beings everywhere adopt ritual attitudes towards the animals and plants in their vicinity. Consider, for example, the separate, and often bizarre, rules which govern the behaviour of Englishmen towards the creatures which they classify as (i) wild animals, (ii) foxes, (iii) game, (iv) farm animals, (v) pets, (vi) vermin. Notice further that if we take the sequence of words; (ia) strangers, (iia) enemies, (iiia) friends, (iva) neighbours, (va) companions, (via) criminals, the two sets of terms are in some degree homologous.[1]

Only the advent of post-Renaissance rational humanism, the invention of 'Man' as an entity separate from nature, concerned to operate logically on it, not co-operate analogically with it, conceals that from us.

For the student of literature, the implications of Lévi-Strauss's sort of 'structural' anthropology and the structural linguistics from which it derives, must be considerable. Primarily, the notions fundamental to both disciplines provide a basis for, and so lend power to, the modern attack on 'realism' or 'naturalism': the presupposition that a transparent 'one-to-one' correspondence exists between a work of art in language, and the 'reality' or 'nature' to which that work of art is

[1] Edmund Leach, *Lévi-Strauss* (London, Fontana, 1970), p. 40.

presupposed to 'refer'. By its undermining of what Lévi-Strauss calls 'sterile empiricism', that is, the notion that the 'real' world consists of a single undeniable reality which, in their ignorance or perversity, the lesser 'savage' minds do not recognize, such anthropology opens the door to the notion that all societies construct their own realities in accordance with mental or psychological principles that determine form and function, and that they then covertly project these upon whatever the real world may in fact be. Its fundamental perception is that this is what all societies do, not just 'primitive' or 'savage' ones. The 'savage' mind, it argues, is the quintessential human mind, operating in a mode that differs from that of the mind of 'civilized' man, but to no different end. The nature of both minds remains, in the last analysis, the same. As a result, this view enables us to see 'civilized' works of art as, in great measure, linked with 'primitive' mythology in their concern to reinforce and uphold the same process: the construction of the world they appear only to describe. That is, it reveals to us, particularly in its account of the nature of myth, the confirming, supportive, problem-resolving nature of all art. It thus strengthens the notion that art acts as a mediating, moulding force in society rather than as an agency which merely reflects or records.

For instance, in Totemism, Lévi-Strauss draws a parallel between the philosopher Bergson's concepts of reality, and those 'common to all the Sioux, from the Osage in the south to the Dakota in the north, according to which things and beings are nothing but materialized forms of creative continuity' (Totemism, p. 171). Reconcilement of perceived opposites has been seen to be the aim of myth and totemism: it is of course also the aim of 'philosophical' thought. Both the philosopher's thinking, and that of the Indian, manifested in totemic systems and myths, show the same desire, says Lévi-Strauss, 'to apprehend in a total fashion the two aspects of reality . . . continuous and discontinuous'. It happens that, in respect of the literary movement called Symbolism, reconcilement of the same 'opposition' with regard to time formed a central preoccupation of poets such as T. S. Eliot. Eliot's feeling that, against our commitment to a notion of sequential, continuously flowing time, there needs to be set a contrary sense of suspended 'discontinuous' moments of time, which are both 'in' time and 'outside' it, receives a brilliant exposition in his Four Quartets:

> Time past and time future
> Allow but a little consciousness.
> To be conscious is not to be in time.
> But only in time can the moment in the rose-garden,
> The moment in the arbour where the rain beat,
> The moment in the draughty church at smokefall
> Be remembered; involved with past and future.
> Only through time time is conquered.

> (*Burnt Norton*)

Lévi-Strauss's arguments in no way 'explain' the character of Eliot's lines, but they do contribute an enlarging dimension to the form of the thought that animates them. If Eliot's contradictory senses of time are strikingly similar (via the philosophy of Bergson, which influenced him) to that of the Sioux nation (Lévi-Strauss quotes from a version of the Indian source):

> Everything as it moves, now and then, here and there, makes stops. The bird as it flies stops in one place to make its nest, and in another to rest in its flight. A man when he goes forth stops when he wills. So the god has stopped . . .

> (*Totemism*, p. 171)

– then what confronts us is rather more complex than the coincidental 'sameness' of the relevant structures. It involves at the very least a resurrection in the sophisticated 'civilized' mind of the 'savage' desire for a totemic reconciliation of the opposition between the ongoing movement of time, and its 'stopped', 'frozen' or 'timeless' moments. It is significant that where the 'civilized' mind aims to achieve this reconciliation through 'art' or 'philosophy', the 'savage' mind aims to achieve it through myth. And we might even add that, in respect of his covert link with the Sioux, the highly Europeanized Eliot remained nevertheless more American than he, or we, had realized.

In short, it confirms that totemism, or 'savage' ways of thinking, far from being the preserve, or the burden, of 'primitive' man, in fact lie dormant in *all* men. The definitive shape of that universal 'human mind' which locates itself in 'savage' as well as in 'civilized' carriers, and is borne indiscriminately by all of us, regardless of time, place or history, emerges clearly in its fictive acts, in its stories, its myths and, it follows, in their 'civilized' counterparts: novels, plays and poems. However apparently firmly rooted in a particular and concrete 'present' and an individual response to it each of these may be, they betray beyond that immediate present and beyond that individual response, the trans-historical and trans-personal imprint that marks them as human constructs. The apparent immediacy and 'concreteness' of writing has always served to conceal this feature, and confirmation of its existence is more readily available in different forms. As a result, both music and mythology, as aural/oral, 'nonliterate' modes of art have the status, in Lévi-Strauss's later work, of highly efficient 'machines for the suppression of time'. That is, they function trans-historically as entities whose non-discursive *forms* give information above and beyond any discursive *content*. Indeed music (and perhaps myth) can perhaps be said to consist *entirely* of form.

But what of literary art? Any view of novels, poems, and to a lesser extent plays, which wishes to respond to them as 'machines for the suppression of time' will ultimately have to concern itself with those aspects of a work which, although rooted in time, have another, prior, 'timeless' level of existence.

Once again, the structuralist impulse can be seen to probe like an x-ray beyond apparently independently existing concrete objects, beyond an 'item-centred' (or 'phonetic') world, into a 'relational' (or 'phonemic') one. With regard to literature this means, initially, pushing beyond mere content into an area which we can loosely term that of form.

3

THE STRUCTURES OF LITERATURE

WHEN we turn our attention directly to literature, it is clear that a concern with form must rank as one of the central 'structuralist' pre-occupations, so that a school of literary criticism which claims to focus attention pre-eminently upon form must consequently be of some interest to us. When in 1965 Tzvetan Todorov published in Paris a selection, translated into French, of the forty-year-old writings of a group of Russian critics under the title of *Théorie de la Littérature*, it attracted considerable notice and has since exerted a good deal of influence. The critics involved had all been members of what was known as the 'Russian Formalist' movement.

RUSSIAN FORMALISM: THE KNIGHT'S MOVE

The name itself was originally applied to a school of literary criticism which flowered in Russia just before and during the 1920s and which was suppressed for political reasons in 1930. Its most widely known proponents were linguists and literary historians such as Boris Eichen-baum, Viktor Shklovsky, Roman Jakobson, Boris Tomasjevsky, Juri Tynyanov, and its two major centres were the Moscow Linguistic Circle (founded 1915), whose members were primarily linguists, and the

Petrograd Society for the Study of Poetic Language (founded 1916) whose members were primarily literary historians. In Russian, the initial letters of the latter society were combined in the acronym OPOYAZ, which became the title given to the formalist movement at large. Early statements of the formalist doctrine are to be found in the Petrograd OPOYAZ symposium *Studies in the Theory of Poetic Language* (1916, enlarged 1917, and then published with new essays by Osip Brik, Eichenbaum and Shklovsky as *Poetics* in 1919), and in Roman Jakobson's *Modern Russian Poetry* (1921).[1]

Early Formalism built on the groundwork of Symbolism, and of the symbolist concern with form as a viable communicative instrument; autonomous, self-expressive, able by extra-verbal rhythmic, associative and connotative means to 'stretch' language beyond its normal 'everyday' range of meaning. These concerns engendered in criticism a preoccupation with the techniques by which literary language works, and a concern to specify and differentiate these from the modes of 'ordinary' language. But, as Eichenbaum wrote, the formalists 'entered the fight against the symbolists in order to wrest poetics from their hands – to free it from its ties with their subjective philosophical and aesthetic theories, and to direct it towards the scientific investigation of facts' (Lemon and Reis, p. 106).

Thus, while it was its opponents who called the OPOYAZ 'formalists' their declared concern with 'objective facts' moved them to prefer the title 'specifiers', and to describe their pursuit as a 'morphological approach' to literature.

As such terms suggest, their preoccupations shared a good deal of common ground with those of the 'structural' linguists and, though they could not have known it, with the 'structural' anthropologists of the future. While their methods differed somewhat, their aims were the same. The formalists felt themselves to be fundamentally concerned

[1] This account of Formalism, like any other, is heavily indebted to the work of Victor Erlich, particularly his definitive study *Russian Formalism*. See also his 'Russian Formalism', *Journal of the History of Ideas*, Vol. 34, No. 4, 1973, pp. 627–38. In addition see the commentary by Fredric Jameson, *The Prison House of Language*, pp. 43 ff.

   The two most easily available collections of Russian Formalist criticism translated into English are Lee T. Lemon and Marion J. Reis (eds.), *Russian Formalist Criticism: Four Essays* and Ladislav Matejka and Krystyna Pomorska (eds.), *Readings in Russian Poetics*.

with literary *structure*: with the recognition, isolation and objective description of the peculiarly literary nature and use of certain 'phonemic' *devices* in the literary work, and not with that work's 'phonetic' content, its 'message', its 'sources', its 'history' or with its sociological, biographical or psychological dimensions. Art, they argued, was autonomous: a permanent, self-determining, continuous human activity which warranted nothing less than examination in and on its own terms. In the words of Shklovsky, 'Art was always free of life and its colour never reflected the colour of the flag which waved over the fortress of the city' (Erlich, p. 77). And if art, and specifically literature, was of this nature, then literary scholarship and criticism should be seen as a distinct and unified intellectual activity, with its proper area of operations clearly and unequivocally defined. In accordance with the general and manifestly 'structural' principle proposed by Shklovsky that 'the forms of art are explainable by the laws of art' (Lemon and Reis, p. 57), that area was emphatically concerned with the 'how' of literature, not the 'what': with the distinctive nature of the literary art in general. To accept Shklovsky's dictum that 'By "works of art", in the narrow sense, we mean works created by special techniques designed to make the works as obviously artistic as possible' (Lemon and Reis, p. 8), is also to accept Jakobson's conclusion that 'The subject of literary scholarship is not literature in its totality but literariness (*literaturnost*) i.e. that which makes of a given work a work of literature' (Erlich, p. 172).

It follows, of course, that those distinguishing structural features would be found within the work itself, not in its author: in the poem, not the poet. And since anything might serve as material for a poem, their location is bound ultimately to be in the distinctive use of language involved, not in any particular topic or concern embodied in the work. Poetry, the formalists insisted, was made out of words, not 'poetic' subjects.

This particular bearing threw emphasis not on the images poets used – indeed the formalists insisted that figurative language, metaphors, symbols, 'visual pictures', far from being prerequisites of poetry were no less characteristic of 'ordinary' language – but on those features of language that were precisely and solely necessary in order to cause literary art to exist. If the 'study of the laws of literary production'

(Erlich, p. 81) was the main concern of the formalist, then in the sphere of literary analysis his interest was likely to be not in the presence of images, but in the use to which these were put.

Indeed, images and all other purely literary devices such as phonetic patterns, rhyme, rhythm, metre, the use of sound not to 'represent' sense, but as a meaningful element in its own right, were assigned by Shklovsky to one central use: that of 'making strange' (*ostranenie*). According to Shklovsky, the essential function of poetic art is to counteract the process of habituation encouraged by routine everyday modes of perception. We very readily cease to 'see' the world we live in, and become anaesthetized to its distinctive features. The aim of poetry is to reverse that process, to *defamiliarize* that with which we are overly familiar, to 'creatively deform' the usual, the normal, and so to inculcate a new, childlike, non-jaded vision in us. The poet thus aims to disrupt 'stock responses', and to generate a heightened awareness: to restructure our ordinary perception of 'reality', so that we end by *seeing* the world instead of numbly recognizing it: or at least so that we end by designing a 'new' reality to replace the (no less fictional) one which we have inherited and become accustomed to. In this, it is worth noting, Russian Formalism pre-dates the Brechtian concept of 'alienation' (*verfremdung*) whereby the object of art is seen to be the revolutionary goal of making the audience aware that the institutions and social formulae which they inherit are not eternal and 'natural' but historical and man-made, and so capable of change through human action.

'Making strange' ranks as a central preoccupation of formalism and a good deal of the most valuable formalist analyses of literature consequently consist of an account of the various means whereby and conditions in which *ostranenie* takes place. It follows that these also constitute an account of the structural means whereby and the conditions in which 'literariness' may be recognized and distinguished from other modes and manners of linguistic communication. For by comparison with 'ordinary' language, literary language not only 'makes' strange, it *is* strange.

The ways and means involved consist in practice of various devices or techniques (*priem*) which act as the agencies of 'literariness', thus constituting the basis of the literary art, the fundamental aim towards which all the elements of literature are organized, and the standard by which they may be judged.

With regard to poetry, this immediately requires that poetic discourse be seen as fundamentally different in its *modus operandi* from discourse of any other kind. In effect, it raises the activities of discourse to a much higher degree than 'normal' language does. Its aim is not simply practical, or cognitive, concerned to transmit information or to formulate knowledge that lies beyond itself. Poetic language is deliberately self-conscious, self-aware. It emphasizes itself as a 'medium' over and above the 'message' it contains: it characteristically draws attention to itself and systematically intensifies its own linguistic qualities. As a result, words in poetry have the status not simply of vehicles for thoughts, but of objects in their own right, autonomous concrete entities. In Saussure's terms, then, they cease to be 'signifiers' and become 'signifieds', and it is the poem's alienating devices of rhythm, rhyme, metre, etc. which enable this structural change to be achieved. As Roman Jakobson puts it, in a statement for which, we shall see later, there is considerable support in his own linguistic theory,

> The distinctive feature of poetry lies in the fact that a word is perceived as a word and not merely a proxy for the denoted object or an outburst of an emotion, that words and their arrangement, their meaning, their outward and inward form acquire weight and value of their own.
>
> (*cit.* Erlich, p. 183)

However, later formalist theory realized that the 'meaning' habitually carried by words can never be fully separated from the words themselves because no word has one 'simple' meaning. The 'meaning' of A is not simply A1 or A2 or A3, for A has a larger capacity to mean which derives from its particular context or use. No word is *ever* really a mere proxy for a denoted object. In fact, the transaction of 'meaning' has a complexity of dimensions which the 'poetic' use of language further complicates. Poetry, in short, does not *separate* a word from its meaning, so much as *multiply* – often bewilderingly – the range of meanings available to it. Again, it raises the degree of normal linguistic activity. A word's 'freedom' from its habitual referent ultimately invokes its potential freedom to combine with an enormous number of referents. In short, a 'poetic' use of a word makes ambiguity a notable feature of its performance, and it is this that alters its structural role from that of signifier to that of signified.

When the devices of versification, patterns of rhyme and rhythm are also considered, it becomes clear that they too contribute inextricably to the range of 'meanings' available, in ways that are determined both externally, by convention, and internally, by the expectations aroused by the poem itself. Thus the sum total of 'devices' employed in the poem generate and so constitute its range of 'meaning'. In the end, the poem *is* its devices, it *is* its form.

Shklovsky goes on to apply the same notion, which admitedly works well with the lyric, to the quite different structure of the novel. Where the lyric is in a sense 'static' in respect of its object, instantaneous in its impact and graspable as a single unity, the novel's commitment to narrative, to movement in and through time, makes it an essentially dynamic and active entity. Shklovsky's awareness of this, and his attempts to deal with it, constitute one of the first attempts at a 'poetics' of fiction, and it is one which, as we shall see, has greatly influenced subsequent structuralist criticism.

The focus, naturally enough, is on the nature of narrative. If the lyric operates the process of 'making strange' on static objects and institutions in what, to use Saussure's term, could be called an *associative*, 'vertical' mode, the overriding necessity of narrative in the novel forces on it a mode appropriate to its investment in temporality: the *syntagmatic*, 'horizontal' mode. Because the novel concerns itself centrally with sequence, with the continuous passage of time, it offers no other pre-existing concrete material on which the process of defamiliarization is able to act. Moreover there are no laws governing the novel as a form separable from its narrative content. Each novel is different, and each invention of content 're-invents' the form of the novel. The same is not true of the short story, which can be reduced to laws. We can, that is to say, identify the non-story, but not the non-novel (see Jameson, *op. cit.*, p. 73 ff).

Shklovsky's concern therefore focuses on that aspect of the novel's narrative structure in which the process of 'making strange' most clearly manifests itself: the plot. He is careful to distinguish between plot and 'story', and the distinction turns out to be one of his most fruitful notions. 'Story' is simply the basic succession of events, the raw material which confronts the artist. Plot represents the distinctive way in which the 'story' is made strange, creatively deformed and defamiliarized (Lemon and Reis, p. 25). So 'plot' can be seen to be as much an organic element of form in the novel as rhyme or rhythm are in the lyric, and it has a decisively formative role. In fact, the 'hero' of a story can be said to be a function of the plot, and is created by it, just as Hamlet, said Shklovsky, is 'created by the technique of the stage' (Erlich p. 241).

Shklovsky's theories (expressed in *On The Theory of Prose*, Moscow, 1925 and 1929) lead ultimately to a series of prescriptions, chief among which is a demand for the suppression of naturalistic 'motivation' in the novel (because it reinforces habitual perception in the reader) and a consequent emphasis on literary self-consciousness and self-reference (which 'defamiliarizes' our perception): in short, to a demand for an artform pre-eminently aware of and sensitive to its own communicative conventions. The archetype of this sort of novel is Sterne's *Tristram Shandy*, which Shklovsky feels able to call 'the most typical novel in world literature' (Lemon and Reis, p. 57), since its main concern is the business of story-telling. In Shklovsky's terms, its plot is about the transformation of its own story into its own plot: it is a novel about itself (and so, in general, a predecessor of modern avant-garde writing).[1]

If the formalists can be seen ultimately to be arguing that everything in a work of art is there primarily 'to permit the work to come into being in the first place' then, as Fredric Jameson argues, we must accept that this represents a 'radical inversion of the priorities of the work of art' which constitutes nothing short of a 'critical revolution'. For its intent is 'to suspend the commonsense view of the work of art as *mimesis* (i.e. possessing content)' and in its place to substitute a notion of the complete dominance of form.[2] Literature seen thus is intrinsically *literary*: a self-sufficient entity, not a 'window' through which other entities can be perceived. Content is a function of literary form, not something separable from it, perceptible beyond it or through it.

[1] Shklovsky's essay on *Tristram Shandy* appears in Lemon and Reis, *op. cit.*, pp. 25–57.
[2] Jameson, *op. cit.*, pp. 82–3.

Indeed, a work only *seems* to have content: in reality 'it speaks only of its own coming into being, of its own construction'.[1]

There is obviously a good deal of truth in this argument, and its manifest similarity to Saussure's view of language as a self-contained, self-justifying structure seems to confirm the central point. As Jameson comments '. . . all literary works, at the same time that they speak the language of reference, also emit a kind of lateral message about their own process of formation. The event of the reading, in other words, only partially obliterates that earlier event of the writing upon which, as in a palimpsest, it is superposed.'[2] However, there is also the question of degree. The process of 'defamiliarization' presupposes and requires the existence of a body of 'familiar' material, which *seems* to have 'content'. If all literary works engage in defamiliarization all of the time, the absence of a familiar norm or 'control' robs the process of any distinction. It doesn't work. A work of fiction can only speak of its own coming into being against a background of speaking of something else.

The full implications of this problem were perhaps best handled in the work of V. I. Propp, whose *Morphology of the Folktale* remains one of the major formalist contributions, and represents a further significant step towards a 'poetics' appropriate to the art of fiction. Propp's concern, in fact, is exactly with the 'norms' by which narrative structures work, the units of 'content' in which they seem to deal, and his attempt at a taxonomy of these retains considerable structural value to the present day, for, like the myth, the fairy tale[3] ranks as an important prototype of all narrative.

As such, in Propp's analysis, the fairy tale is seen primarily to embody a syntagmatic, 'horizontal' structuring, rather than the associative 'vertical' structuring represented by the lyric. Propp's analysis, in short, reinforces the view that narrative is fundamentally syntagmatic in mode. But the major breakthrough represented in his work derives

[1] Jameson, *op. cit.*, p. 89.

[2] *Ibid.*, p. 89.

[3] Propp's concern is specifically with the *fairy* tale: the use of 'folk-tale' in the title of his study arises from an ambiguity inherent in the word *skazki* which translators have been unable to resolve. See V. Propp, *Morphology of the Folktale*, trans. Laurence Scott, second edition, revised and edited by Louis A. Wagner, p. ix.

from his insistence that in the fairy tale the all-important and unifying element is found, not on a quasi-'phonetic' level, within the 'characters' who appear in the story, but on a 'phonemic' level, in the characters' *function*; the part they play in the *plot*.

If by 'function' is understood 'an act of a character defined from the point of view of its significance for the course of the action' (Propp, p. 21) then it is clear that Propp's position is truly a structuralist one. His argument, based on exhaustive analysis of a large number of tales, leads to the conclusion that the fairy tale characteristically 'often attributes identical actions to various personages' (Propp, p. 20). This makes possible an analysis of the tales according to the various functions of their *dramatis personae*, and this indicates that in fact, despite the surface profusion of detail, 'the number of functions is extremely small, whereas the number of personages is extremely large' (Propp, p. 20). Hence the phenomenon of 'duplicity' which Lévi-Strauss notes in the structures of myth, and its curious effect on the language involved: the 'two-fold quality of a tale: its amazing multiformity, picturesqueness and colour, and on the other hand its no less striking uniformity, its repetition' (Propp, pp. 20–1).

Analysis of these elements of uniformity and repetition leads Propp to the conclusion that all fairy tales are structurally homogeneous, and embody the following basic principles:

1   Functions of characters serve as stable, constant elements in a tale, independently of how and by whom they are fulfilled. They constitute the fundamental components of a tale.
2   The number of functions known to the fairy tale is limited (Propp lists and analyses each one: a total of thirty-one functions).[1]
3   The sequence of functions is always identical.
4   All fairy tales are of one type in regard to their structure.

The thirty-one functions, Propp finds, are distributed among seven 'spheres of action' corresponding to their 'respective performers' as follows:

[1] Propp, pp. 26–63.

1 the villain
2 the donor (provider)
3 the helper
4 the princess (a sought-for person) and her father
5 the dispatcher
6 the hero
7 the false hero.

In a specific fairy tale, one character may be involved in several spheres of action, and several characters may be involved in the same sphere of action. But the important thing to notice is that the *number* of spheres of action occuring in the fairy tale is finite: we are dealing with discernible and repeated *structures* which, if they are characteristic of so deeply rooted a form of narrative expression may, as we shall see, have implications for *all* narrative.

A central tenet of formalism was that the vitality of the process of art depended on its 'devices' being seen in action. And by 'baring the devices', by calling attention to the 'defamiliarizing' techniques he is himself drawing upon as he writes, the literary artist is able to gain access to the major overriding device of all: the alienating sense of being thereby made privy to the process by which art works. Thus Tomashevsky cites the extent to which writers conceal or 'bare' their devices as an index of style. There is a nineteenth-century style 'distinguished by its attempt to conceal the device; all of its motivation systems are designed to make the literary devices seem imperceptible, to make them seem as natural as possible – that is, to develop the literary material so that its development is unperceived' (Lemon and Reis, p. 94) – and there is also another style 'an unrealistic style which does not bother about concealing the devices and which frequently tries to make them obvious, as when a writer interrupts a speech he is reporting to say that he did not hear how it ended, only to go on and report what he has no realistic way of knowing. In such a case, the author has called attention to the device or – as they say – the technique is 'laid bare'. Pushkin, in the fourth chapter of *Eugeny Onegin* writes:

And here already sparkle the snows
And they spread among silver fields –

(The reader waits for a rhyme like rose;
Let him take quickly what this poem yields)'.

(*Ibid.*, p. 94)

In essence, this overriding device of alienation has one main purpose, to shock us out of the anaesthetic grip our language maintains on our perceptions. As we have already seen, Saussure points out that native speakers tend to assume a necessary 'fitness', an unquestionable 'identity' between signifier and signified, between the 'sound image' made by the word 'tree', and the concept of an actual tree. This assumption is the basis of language's anaesthetic function.

But, as Jakobson argues, the poet's job – as one who works with language in the way that a painter works with colour – requires him to refuse to permit that anaesthetic to operate: 'The function of poetry is to point out that the sign is not identical with its referent' (Erlich, p. 181). And so what is important in any poem is not the poet's or the reader's attitude to reality, but the poet's attitude towards *language* which, when successfully communicated, 'wakes up' the reader, and makes him see the structure of his language, and so that of his 'world', anew.

Thus, for Jakobson and other formalists, the differentiating quality of 'literariness' resides ultimately in the poet's distinctive use of language. Poetic language, as we shall see when we consider Jakobson's linguistic theory, becomes a kind of specially intensified language in which signifiers act as signifieds, and which operates through its own internal laws, appropriate to and reflective of its own nature. The repetition of sound and rhythmic structures characteristic of poetry, and embodied in conventionalized *formulae* such as rhyme, alliteration and metre, have therefore no reference to a 'reality' beyond the poem, but derive (as even *onomatopoeia* does) from conventions arising within the particular language involved. They act as auxiliary devices signalling the 'organized character' of poetic language (Erlich, p. 214).

Thus, formalists like Brik who were concerned to analyse such elements, treated the poem as an intrinsic and self-regulating structure in which rhyme has a similar status to metaphor: it also 'deforms and modifies' meaning, and brings potential, 'lateral' meanings into play. Poetry seen thus becomes, according to Jakobson, a deliberate 'deformation' of ordinary language: it is 'organized violence committed on ordinary speech' (Erlich, p. 219).

By extension, literature at large can be seen as a special kind of activity: one which, albeit permanent, and wholly natural to the human species, is nevertheless isolatable, separable from what goes on beyond it, and thus, like language itself, perceivable as a structure, in exactly the terms we have encountered earlier, advocated by Piaget: whole, capable of transformation, self-regulating, autonomous and internally coherent. And literary change can be seen, not as a response to, or a by-product of social change, but as the unfolding of a self-generating and self-enclosed sequence of styles and genres, propelled and furthered by internal exigencies.

And so a new 'formalist' version of literary history becomes possible, in which new forms or styles emerge in revolt against the old, but not as their antithesis, so much as a reorganization, a regrouping, of permanent elements. This is also part of the process of *ostranenie*: when the 'strange' becomes itself habitual, it needs to be replaced.

In this process, parody has an important role to play, since it always uses another literary work as background, 'takes off' from that by laying bare its 'devices'. As Erlich puts it 'the obsolete device is not thrown overboard, but repeated in a new incongruous context and thus . . . made "perceptible" again' (Erlich, p. 258). The process indicates literature's permanent self-consciousness, and its continuous need for self-appraisal and realignment. In fact, Shklovsky went so far as to propound a 'law' purporting to account for the process of literary realignment whose central principle was the 'canonization of the junior branch'. In order to renew itself, he argued, literature periodically redraws its own boundaries, so as to include from time to time elements, motifs and devices regarded until then as 'peripheral' or 'junior' in relation to the 'main stream' of literary endeavour. Thus sub-literary or 'junior' genres such as journalism, vaudeville, the detective story, find aspects of themselves drawn into the 'canon' of official literature.

In short, the 'law' implies that all art exists in a continuum, that 'high' art periodically shifts its boundaries within that continuum in order to renew itself, and that the only constant in this process is the sense which 'literature' must always manifest, of being 'literary'. In other words, what *defines* literature in any age is its *structural* role: its 'opposition' to the non-literature of that age.

It is this notion of literature as a kind of *langue*, an autonomous, internally coherent, self-limiting, self-regulating, self-justifying structure, which centrally animates formalist criticism and links it clearly with 'structural' developments in linguistics and anthropology. The individual work of art stands as a sort of *parole* in relation to its parent *langue*, a relationship in which each illuminates and is illuminated by the other. In short, *conventionality*, the operation of tacit unquestioned structural 'rules', emerges as the animating principle of literary art. Whether that art has pretensions towards 'realism' or not, it remains as 'bound' by conventions which act as rules as much as a game of chess does. We have already noted Saussure's analogy between chess and language as autonomous 'structures'. The peculiarities of the way in which the knight is required to move in that game have nothing to do with any 'reality' outside the game, and require no external validation. The knight's move can thus stand as an appropriate symbol for Formalism's pervasive preoccupation: the relation of the rules, not to 'reality', but to the game itself. It is thus fitting that one of Viktor Shklovsky's volumes should be called *Xod Konja*, or *The Knight's Move*, and that in it he should apologize for what Erlich calls the 'tortuous quality' of his criticism with the following plea: 'There are many reasons for the oddity of the knight's move, but the principal reason is the conventionality of art. I write about the conventions in art' (Erlich, pp. 190–1).

EUROPEAN STRUCTURAL LINGUISTICS

The Russian political climate of the 1930s ultimately proved altogether hostile to the formalist movement, and it was finally suppressed. However, by that time, some of its most important theoretical elements had taken root and blossomed in the field of structural linguistics, which, as we have already noticed above, was beginning to develop independently on both sides of the Atlantic.

Attention has already been drawn to the commitment of American linguists to the construction of synchronic accounts of native Indian languages, a commitment arising partly from their fear that to describe these 'exotic' languages in terms of familiar Indo-European categories could have a distorting effect on them. And we have remarked that this practice eventually led to the development of an inherently 'structural' view of language and culture whose major proponents, Boas, Sapir, Whorf and later Bloomfield, produced influential work in the field of what has come to be termed 'descriptive linguistics'.

Meanwhile, in Europe, two significant centres of linguistic study had developed following the death of Saussure, and they are both important in respect of the growth and expansion of structuralism. These were the Prague (or 'functional') school, represented most effectively by the work of Nikolay Trubetskoy and the erstwhile formalist Roman Jakobson (both emigrés from Russia), and the Copenhagen (or 'glossematic') school, best represented by the work of Louis Hjelmslev. These three varieties of linguistic study, *descriptive, functional, glossematic* constitute the major 'structuralist' modes of linguistic analysis current in the twentieth century.

Copenhagen structuralism manifested itself in the emphasis Hjelmslev placed on the *formal* nature of all language: 'it would seem to be a generally valid thesis that for every *process* there is a corresponding *system* by which the process can be analyzed and described by means of a limited number of premises.'[1] Accordingly, he set himself the task of constructing a 'calculus' capable of providing the 'tools for describing or comprehending a given text and the language on which it is constructed'.[2]

As for the Prague school, as Victor Erlich says, structuralism was their 'battle cry'. The most characteristic feature of their approach was the combination of the central notion that language was to be seen as an ultimately coherent structure, not as an aggregate of isolated entities, with a recognition and analysis of the variety of 'functions' that it fulfils in society. Thus the *cognitive* or *referential* function of language operates when it is used for the transmission of information; the *expressive* or *emotive* function is seen when language is used to indicate the mood or attitude of the speaker, or the writer; the *conative* or *injunctive*

---

[1] Louis Hjelmslev, *Prologomena to a Theory of Language* (University of Wisconsin Press, Madison, Wisconsin, 1961), p. 9.

[2] See B. Trnka and others, 'Prague structural linguistics' in Michael Lane, ed., *Structuralism: a reader*, pp. 73–4.

function is involved when it is used to influence the person to whom it is addressed, and there are also *phatic* and *metalingual* functions. We shall be looking at these again when we consider the work of Roman Jakobson more closely.

In respect of the literary use of language, the distinction between cognitive and expressive functions was applied by the Prague school linguists, as we shall see, to formulate the principle that language is being used 'poetically' or 'aesthetically' when its expressive aspect is dominant: that is, when its language deviates maximally from 'normal' usage, by means of devices which thrust the act of expression itself into the foreground. As the Czech linguist Jan Mukařovský puts it, this act of 'foregrounding' (an English version of the term *aktualisace*) is crucial:

> The function of poetic language consists in the maximum of fore-grounding of the utterance . . . it is not used in the services of com-munication, but in order to place in the foreground the act of expres-sion, the act of speech itself.[1]

In other words, there can be said to exist a sixth, *poetic* or *aesthetic* function of language which manifests itself in the form of an utterance, not merely in the 'meaning' or 'content' of its separate words. The interest in form implied by these functions enabled the Prague linguists to salvage the healthy elements of the OPOYAZ doctrines and to pro-mote Formalism in terms of what Erlich calls 'the close co-operation of linguistics and poetics' (Erlich, p. 158).

That co-operation eventually pushed Formalism into the much larger field of signification in general. For, seen through the eyes of the 'functional' linguist, 'Everything in the work of art, and in its relation to the outside world . . . can be discussed in terms of sign and meaning . . . aesthetics can be regarded as a part of the modern science of signs' (Mukařovský, cit. Erlich, p. 159). We shall be returning to the notion of a larger 'science of signs' later, but it is important to notice now that, in such a context, the 'restricted' formalist view of poetics can no longer

---

[1] Jan Mukařovský, 'Standard language and poetic language' in *A Prague School Reader on Aesthetics, Literary Structure and Style* selected and translated by Paul L. Garvin, Washington, D.C.: Georgetown University Press, 1964, pp. 43–4.

be binding. If the 'aesthetic' aspect of language operates as a valid function within a total system which includes all aspects of communication, then many of the formalist preoccupations with 'literariness' must become integrated into the larger concerns of structural linguistics. The crucial figure central to the Prague school's efforts in this sphere is undoubtedly that of Roman Jakobson.

ROMAN JAKOBSON

Jakobson's approach to poetry is essentially that of the linguist, and 'poetics' for him forms part of the general field of linguistics. As a formalist, one of his major interests lies of course in the attempt to give an account of the poetic function of language, but this is pursued under the larger umbrella of a comprehensive linguistic theory. To this end, he postulates two general linguistic notions which help to focus on the particular character of language when it is used poetically: the notion of polarities, and the notion of equivalence.

Jakobson's concept of 'polarities' in language derives from Saussure's insight concerning the syntagmatic and associative planes of linguistic performance, and it confirms the notion of the 'sparking' force of binary opposition even at that basic level. Writing in 1956 about the linguistic problems of the disorder called *aphasia*[1] (loss or impairment of the power to understand and to use speech), Jakobson records his observation that the two major (and binarily opposed) component disorders ('similarity disorder' and 'contiguity disorder') seem to be strikingly related to the two basic rhetorical figures metaphor and metonymy.

Both are figures of 'equivalence' in that they characteristically propose a different entity as having 'equivalent' status to the one that forms the main subject of the figure. Thus, in the metaphor 'the car beetled along', the movement of a beetle is proposed as 'equivalent' to that of the car, and in the metonymic phrase 'The White House considers a new policy', a specific building is proposed as 'equivalent' to the president of the United States. Broadly speaking, metaphor is based on a proposed similarity or analogy between the literal subject (the

---

[1] Roman Jakobson and Morris Halle, *Fundamentals of Language*, pp. 69–96.

car's movement) and its metaphorical substitute (the beetle's move-ment), whereas metonymy is based on a proposed contiguous (or 'sequential') association between the literal subject (the president) and its 'adjacent' replacement (where the president lives). Metaphor, to apply Saussure's concepts, is generally 'associative' in character and exploits language's 'vertical' relations, where metonymy is generally 'syntagmatic' in character, and exploits language's 'horizontal' relations.

Jakobson sees metaphor and metonymy as the characteristic modes of binarily opposed polarities which between them underpin the two-fold process of *selection* and *combination* by which linguistic signs are formed: 'the given utterance (message) is a *combination* of constituent parts (sentences, words, phonemes, etc.) *selected* from the repository of all possible constituent parts (the code)' (*Fundamentals of Language*, p. 75). Thus messages are constructed, as Saussure said, by a combination of a 'horizontal' movement, which combines words together, and a 'verti-cal' movement, which selects the particular words from the available inventory or 'inner storehouse' of the language. The combinative (or syntagmatic) process manifests itself in contiguity (one word being placed next to another) and its mode is *metonymic*. The selective (or associative) process manifests itself in similarity (one word or concept being 'like' another) and its mode is *metaphoric*. The 'opposition' of metaphor and metonymy therefore may be said to represent in effect the essence of the total opposition between the *synchronic* mode of language (its immediate, coexistent, 'vertical' relationships) and its *diachronic* mode (its sequential, successive, linearly progressive relationships).

Jakobson's study of *aphasia* makes the significant claim that in the patient suffering from 'similarity' disorder, only the *syntagmatic* or com-binative aspects of language seemed to be preserved, and there was a consequent inability to deal in 'associative' relationships, such as 'nam-ing', the use of synonyms, definitions – i.e. the raw material of meta-phors. However, such patients employed *metonymy* widely: they would substitute *fork* for knife, *table* for lamp, *smoke* for fire etc. Meanwhile, in the patient suffering from 'contiguity' disorder, the reverse situation pertained. The 'syntactical rules organizing words into higher units are lost' (p. 85), and the patient's speech was largely confined to the *substitution* of words by 'similarities . . . of a metaphoric nature' (p. 86). Thus, it appears that 'Metaphor is alien to the similarity disorder, and metonymy to the contiguity disorder' (p. 90). As a result it becomes possible to propose that human language in fact does exist in terms of the two fundamental dimensions suggested by Saussure and, moreover, that these dimensions crystallize into the rhetorical devices on which poetry characteristically and preeminently draws. The two axes may be represented as follows:

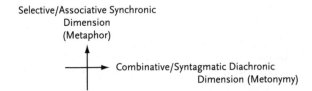

Both metaphor and metonymy can be subdivided into other figures (simile is a type of metaphor; synecdoche is a type of metonymy) but the distinction between the two modes remains fundamental, because it is a product of the fundamental modes of language itself: it is how language works.

Jakobson's most famous formulation on this basis is his definition of the *poetic* function of language as one which draws on both the selective and the combinative modes as a means for the promotion of *equivalence*: 'The poetic function projects the principle of equivalence from the axis of selection into the axis of combination.'[1] This becomes the distinguishing 'trademark' of the 'poetic' use of language, as opposed to any other use. When I say 'my car beetles along' I *select* 'beetles' from a 'storehouse' of possibilities which includes, say, 'goes', 'hurries', 'scurries' etc. and *combine* it with 'car' on the principle that this will make the car's movement and the insect's movement *equivalent*. As Jakobson puts it, 'similarity superimposed on contiguity imparts to poetry its thoroughgoing symbolic, multiplex, polysemantic essence . . . Said more technically, anything sequent is a simile. In poetry where

---

[1] Roman Jakobson, 'Closing statement: linguistics and poetics' in Thomas A. Sebeok, ed., *Style in Language*, p. 358.

similarity is superinduced upon contiguity, any metonymy is slightly metaphorical and any metaphor has a metonymical tint'.[1]

Jakobson is also prepared to consider a preference for one mode or the other as a kind of rough and ready index of literary style:

> The primacy of the metaphoric process in the literary schools of romanticism and Symbolism has been repeatedly acknowledged, but it is still insufficiently realized that it is the predominance of metonymy which underlies and actually predetermines the so-called 'realistic' trend . . .[2]

In fact, he argues that a universal 'competition' between both modes will be manifested in any symbolic process or system of signs, be it intrapersonal or social, and instances that of painting where it is possible to distinguish between Cubism as metonymic and Surrealism as metaphoric in mode. Structuralist psycho-analysts such as Jacques Lacan have even suggested that these two modes of symbolic representation provide a model for the understanding of psychic functions: the concept of metaphor illuminates the notion of 'symptom' (the replacing of one signifier by an associated one), that of metonymy sheds light on the origin of desire (through the combinative connection of signifier to signifier and the sense this implies of the infinite extension of such a process into uncharted areas).[3]

Jakobson's 'polarities' thus seem to take us to the heart of the act of signification itself and in so doing to suggest very important ways in which modes of signification may be distinguished from each other. True to his formalist background, his concern centres on the ways in which poetry differs from prose, and in which 'literariness' in language marks itself as distinctive.

We have already noticed the argument of Jakobson's fellow Prague school critic Mukařovský with regard to 'foregrounding': that the

---

[1] 'Closing statement', *op. cit.*, p. 370.

[2] *Fundamentals of Language*, pp. 91–2.

[3] See A. G. Wilden, *The Language of the Self* (Baltimore: Johns Hopkins Press, 1968), p. 114, and Fredric Jameson, *The Prison-House of Language*, p. 122. Cf. Jakobson's remarks on Freud and Frazer, *Fundamentals of Language*, p. 95.

'aesthetic' use of language pushes into the foreground the 'act of expression' itself. Jakobson offers the more refined proposal that the metaphoric mode tends to be foregrounded in poetry, whereas the metonymic mode tends to be foregrounded in prose. This makes the operation of 'equivalence' of crucial importance to poetry, not only in the area of analogy, but also in the area of 'sound'; of those metrical, rhythmic and phonic devices whose promotion of a sense of repeated 'sameness', of *pattern*, constitutes the *raison d'être* of verse:

> The principle of similarity underlies poetry; the metrical parallelism of lines, or the phonic equivalence of rhyming words prompts the question of semantic similarity and contrast . . . Prose, on the contrary, is forwarded essentially by contiguity. Thus, for poetry, metaphor, and for prose, metonymy is the line of least resistance . . .'

By the use of complex inter-relationships, by emphasizing resemblances and by promoting through repetition 'equivalences' or 'parallelisms' of sound, stress, image, rhyme, poetry patterns and 'thickens' language, 'foregrounding' its formal qualities, and consequently 'backgrounding' its capacity for sequential, discursive and referential meaning. Words similar in sound are 'drawn together in meaning'; ambiguity is consequently favoured, and equivalence is promoted to the status of a 'constitutive device' of the art. Poetry thus resides not in the mere adornment of 'ordinary' language: it represents almost the construction of a different *kind* of language: 'poeticalness is not a supplementation of discourse with rhetorical adornment but a total re-evaluation of the discourse and of all its components whatsoever'.[2]

It is worth stressing, however, that in Jakobson's theory 'poeticalness' appears as an aspect of *all* uses of language and cannot simply be confined to poetry. In short, the 'poetic function' forms part of the way all language works, and is not just a special set of 'tricks' that poets perform. Poetry only occurs, it follows, when 'poeticalness' is raised to a higher degree than any of the other competing functions, although they will obviously all continue to operate. Thus:

[1] *Fundamentals of Language*, pp. 95–6.
[2] 'Closing statement', p. 377.

> Poetic function is not the sole function of verbal art, but only its dominant, determining function, whereas in all other verbal activities it acts as a subsidiary, accessory constituent. This function, by promoting the palpability of signs, deepens the fundamental dichotomy of signs and objects. Hence, when dealing with poetic function, linguistics cannot limit itself to the field of poetry.[1]

Of course, we have methods of analyzing poetry which are more or less satisfactory in that they can more or less deal with the metaphorical nature of the material. But the analysis of prose is less well advanced:

> . . . so-called realistic literature, intimately tied with the metonymic principle, still defies interpretation, although the same linguistic methodology, which poetics uses when analyzing the metaphorical style of romantic poetry, is entirely applicable to the metonymical texture of realistic prose.[2]

What we need, Jakobson concludes, is therefore a *poetics* of both poetry *and* prose which will attend to the differential, contrastive functioning of metaphor and metonymy at all levels.

The notion of a 'poetics' for prose will recur in our account of subsequent structuralist proposals for the analysis of fiction, but so far never fully developed along the lines suggested by Jakobson. This perhaps comes about because although Jakobson appears to be offering a method of analysis, in fact, as Jonathan Culler has suggested, his work largely constitutes 'a hypothesis about the conventions of poetry as an institution, and in particular about the kind of attention to language which poets and readers are allowed to assume'.[3] That is, Jakobson is talking about our response, as members of a community, to poetry and to prose, rather than about poetry and prose *per se*.

Part of the difficulty lies of course in the fact that poetry and prose do not exist *per se*. Their nature is determined by the conventional role society gives to the particular uses of language in which they engage.

---

[1] 'Closing statement', p. 356.

[2] 'Closing statement', p. 375.

[3] Jonathan Culler, *Structuralist Poetics*, p. 69.

Jakobson's work on the nature of the communicative act, and on the *functions* of the language involved has already been mentioned. His account of the 'poetic function' has been of particular significance. It confirms the insights already mentioned, and supplies the theoretical basis for the final stage of the bridge which links Formalism and Structuralism in respect of literature.

Very briefly, Jakobson draws attention to the six constituent factors that make up any speech event. These can be best understood by means of his diagram[1]:

```
                        context
                        message
        addresser------------------------------------ addressee
                        contact
                        code
```

All communication consists of a *message* initiated by an *addresser*, whose destination is an *addressee*. But the process is not as simple as that. The message requires a *contact* between addresser and addressee, which may be oral, visual, electronic or whatever. It must be formulated in terms of a *code*: speech, numbers, writing, sound-formations etc. And the message must refer to a *context* understood by both addresser and addressee, which enables the message to 'make sense' – as (we hope) the context of the present discussion enables individual phrases and sentences to be meaningful where otherwise (uttered at, say, a football match) they would not.

The central point to emerge from Jakobson's account of communication is that the 'message' does not and cannot supply all of the 'meaning' of the transaction, and that a good deal of what is communicated derives from the context, the code, and the means of contact. 'Meaning' in short resides in the *total* act of communication, a situation intensified by the fact that all languages contain grammatical elements which have no precise meaning *per se*, and which are wholly sensitive in this respect to the *context* in which they occur. That is, their meaning is capable of considerable degrees of change, depending on how they are used, and where they occur.

[1] 'Closing statement', p. 353.

Such units are called 'shifters' and in English this refers to words such as 'I', 'you', 'me' and so on. The actual *person* these words *mean* is of course entirely dependent on the particular message which contains them. They are totally context-sensitive, and 'distinguished from all other constituents of the linguistic code solely by their compulsory reference to the given message'.[1] What 'shifters' indicate, of course, is the extent to which *all* meaning is context-sensitive, and the limited access to so-called 'General Meaning' that any communication can have. The importance of this (with particular reference to the use of the 'shifting' perspective involved in the personal pronoun) will be emphasized when we consider some of the French structuralist accounts of fictional prose, and in particular their attack on the idea of an 'un-shifting' or 'unitary' meaning available to the reader. The 'meaning' offered by any use of language, as seen, say, by Roland Barthes, not only characteristically 'shifts', but can (and should) be 'shifted'.

'Meaning' then, according to Jakobson's account, is not a stable, predetermined entity which passes, untrammelled, from sender to receiver. The very nature of language prohibits this, as does the fact that the six elements involved in the transmission process are never in perfect 'balance'. One or other of them is always dominant to a greater or lesser extent over the others. Thus, the communication may find itself orientated towards the *context* in one situation, or the *code* in another, or the *contact* in yet another, and so on.

True to the functional commitment of his Prague school background, Jakobson goes on to argue that each of the six elements involved in the communication event has a distinct functional role. The nature of the message is finally determined by the fact that it takes on the functional character of whichever of the six elements involved happens to be dominant. To understand this, we need to supply to the above diagram of the speech event, the following additional functional dimensions[2]:

---

[1] Roman Jakobson, 'Shifters, verbal categories, and the Russian verb' in *Selected Writings* Vol. II, p. 132.

[2] 'Closing statement', p. 357.

<table>
<tr><td></td><td>referential</td><td></td></tr>
<tr><td></td><td>poetic</td><td></td></tr>
<tr><td>emotive</td><td></td><td>conative</td></tr>
<tr><td></td><td>phatic</td><td></td></tr>
<tr><td></td><td>metalingual</td><td></td></tr>
</table>

This means that if the communication is orientated towards *context*, then the *referential* function dominates, and this determines the general character of a message such as 'The distance from Cardiff to London is one hundred and fifty miles' which aims to refer to a context beyond itself, and to convey concrete, objective information about that. This seems to be the leading task of most messages, of course, but the matter cannot simply be left there. For instance, if the communication is orientated towards the *addresser* of the message, then the *emotive* function dominates, and this arrangement would yield a message such as 'London is a long way from home' which aims to express the addresser's emotional response to a particular situation, rather than a purely referential description of it. Similarly, if the communication is angled towards the receiver of the message, the addressee, then the *conative* (or vocative, or imperative) function dominates, indicated by the use of devices such as 'Look!' or 'Listen!' or 'Now see here . . .' or 'I say . . .'. If the communication inclines towards the *contact*, then the *phatic* function dominates (the purpose of this is to check that the contact is working properly: in utterance it yields 'phatic' events such as 'good morning', 'how are you' etc., whose purpose is not to elicit or offer information, but to establish linguistic contact, or to 'prime the pump' of conversation: most British conversation about the weather has this 'phatic' function, rather than a meterological one). If towards the *code*, then the *metalingual* function dominates (this is to check that the same code is being used by both parties: in utterance this yields phrases such as 'understand?', 'see?', 'Get it?', 'O.K.?'). Finally, if the communication is orientated towards the *message* for its own sake, then the *poetic* or *aesthetic* function can be said to be dominant.

In this last instance, Jakobson's comprehensive (and fundamentally structural) view of the way language operates confirms and reinforces that crucial insight into the nature of verbal art to which attention has already been drawn in our assessment of his work as a formalist. For it is of the distinctive essence of the aesthetic use of language, seen thus 'functionally' and in relation to the totality of human communication, that it is *self*-conscious; concerned *above all* to draw attention to its *own nature*, its own sound-patterns, diction, syntax etc. and *not* to refer primarily to some 'reality' beyond itself. Language's 'poetic' function, it will be remembered, promotes 'the palpability of signs'. As a result it systematically undermines the sense of any 'natural' or 'transparent' connection between signifier and signified, sign and object. As Jakobson says, it 'deepens the fundamental dichotomy of signs and objects'.[1] Verbal art, seen thus, is not referential in mode, and does not function as a transparent 'window' through which the reader encounters the poem's or the novel's 'subject'. Its mode is auto-referential; it is its own subject.

As we have already noted in respect of Formalism, and as we shall certainly note again in respect of Structuralism as this is presented by its French propounders, this view of literary art serves to reintegrate form and content, and to present the work, not as the 'container' of a message, but as an intrinsic, self-generating, self-regulating and ultimately self-regarding whole, needing no reference beyond its own boundaries to validate its nature. It is, in short, in Piaget's terms, a structure. In its formulation of a comprehensive theory of language and communication in which this notion of literature has an integral part, Jakobson's work emerges as the bridge linking Formalism and Structuralism, and as the theoretical foundation of both.

In effect, Jakobson's influence has been most strongly felt in the efforts that have been made to apply structural linguistics to the analysis of poetry. But what of prose? Here the linking figure is probably that of Propp, and his heirs are undoubtedly a large and expanding group of French structuralist critics whose work has been given increasing currency in the last ten years. Of these, it seems helpful to look relatively closely at three who may stand as representative of significant developments in the analysis of the structures of fiction, the 'grammar' of plot, the devices which signal to us that we are in the presence of narrative: the constituents, in short, of the elusive 'poetics of prose'.

They can be termed 'structuralist' critics, not because they belong to a particular 'school', but because the essence of their work derives

[1] 'Closing statement', p. 356.

from the principle that literature offers the most obvious manifestation of structuralism in action: that, as Roland Barthes puts it, 'structuralism, itself developed from a linguistic model, finds in literature, which is the work of language, an object that has much more than an affinity with it: the two are homogenous'.[1] And the questions they confront are fundamental ones: how should we define narrative? what are the basic units of fiction? how are these structured?

A. J. GREIMAS

A. J. Greimas is primarily interested in semantics, and his 'structuralist' approach to the matter of meaning has produced two influential books, *Sémantique Structurale*, 1966, and *Du Sens*, 1970. In essence, his work attempts to describe narrative structure in terms of an established linguistic model derived from the Saussurean notion of an underlying *langue* or competence which generates a specific *parole* or performance, as well as from Saussure's and Jakobson's concept of the fundamental signifying role of binary opposition.

Just as the phonemic structure of a language rests on the principle that a sound's function is determined by what it is *phonemically* felt to 'oppose' as much as by what it actually, *phonetically* is, so our fundamental concepts of 'meaning' present themselves to us through the opposition we feel to exist between basic 'semes' or semantic units. Thus, 'dark' is defined principally by our sense of its opposition to 'light', and 'up' by our sense of its opposition to 'down'. The same binary patterning of mutual opposition manifests itself in concepts such as male: female, vertical: horizontal, human: animal etc. As we have seen, contrastive orderings of this sort form the basis of what Lévi-Strauss has termed the 'socio-logic' of the human mind, which structures nature in its own image, and thus establishes the foundation for the systems of totemic 'transformations' that overtly or covertly underpin our picture of the world.

In fact, Greimas argues, the perception of oppositions underlies what he terms the 'elementary structure of signification' on which his

---

[1] Roland Barthes, 'Science versus literature', *The Times Literary Supplement*, 28 September 1967.

semantic theories rest. 'We perceive differences' he writes, 'and thanks to that perception, the world "takes shape" in front of us, and for our purposes' (*Sémantique Structurale*, p. 19). The differences we discern between these basic 'semes' involve, at an elementary level, four terms, seen as two opposed pairs, which our 'structuring' perception requires us to recognize in the following form: A is opposed to B as − A is to − B. In short, the 'elementary structure' involves recognition and distinction of two aspects of an entity: its opposite and its negation. We see B as the opposite of A and − B as the opposite of − A, but we also see − A as the negation of A and − B as the negation of B.[1]

The nature and power of these structures prove in effect so deep and formative that they ultimately shape the elements of our language, its syntax, and the experiences which these articulate in the form of narrative. In effect, Greimas argues, these binary oppositions form the basis of a deep-lying 'actantial model' (*modèle actantiel*) from whose structure the superficial surface structures of individual stories derive, and by which they are generated. The parallel with Saussure's notion of a *langue* which underlies *parole*, and with Chomsky's notion of a competence which precedes performance is clear. Man is the Talking Animal: he is *homo loquens*. So, the fundamental structures of his language must inevitably inform and shape the fundamental structures of his stories. And even though those stories seem different on the surface, a 'structural' analysis reveals that they spring from a common 'grammar' or (to use the term which Greimas employs to give the sense of the model's fundamentally dramatic, interlocutory nature) 'enunciation-spectacle' (*énoncé-spectacle*): 'the content of the actions changes all the time, the actors vary, but the enunciation-spectacle remains always the same, for its permanence is guaranteed by the fixed distribution of the roles'.[2]

At the surface level, the structure of the enunciation-spectacle is manifested through the various *actants* who embody it, as *parole* to its *langue*. To modify the metaphor, these *actants* have a kind of phonemic, rather than a phonetic role: they operate on the level of function, rather

---

[1] *Sémantique Structurale*, pp. 18–29; *Du Sens*, pp. 135–55. See Fredric Jameson, *The Prison-House of Language*, pp. 163–5 for an account and assessment of the intricacies involved.

[2] *Sémantique Structurale*, p. 173.

than content. That is, an *actant* may embody itself in a particular character (termed an *acteur*) or it may reside in the function of more than one character in respect of their common role in the story's underlying 'oppositional' structure. In short, the deep structure of the narrative generates and defines its *actants* at a level beyond that of the story's surface content. As a result, as Jameson puts it, 'it may turn out that a character or actor in a given narrative in reality serves as a cover for two separate and relatively independent *actants*; or that two actors, independent personalities and separate characters in the story-line, amount to little more than alternating articulations of an *actant* structurally identical in both contexts.'[1]

This is not an unfamiliar notion, of course, to Anglo-American criticism. A reasonably modern 'thematic' approach to Shakespeare's plays would have little difficulty, for instance, in accepting that in *King Lear*, the separate 'characters' (*acteurs*) of Cordelia and The Fool in fact embody the same 'theme' (intuitive innocence, set against Lear's rational corruption) and so function as the same *actant*. The account of how Lear himself, by finally embracing their 'foolish' principles, also becomes an aspect of the same *actant*, is of course the story of the play.

But Greimas's quarry is not the elucidation of individual works of literature, so much as the nature of the 'grammar' which generates them. He begins, as we have seen, with the fundamental notion of binary opposition as the basic human conceptual mode. A narrative sequence embodies this mode by the employment of two actants whose relationship must be either oppositional or its reverse; and on the surface level this relationship will therefore generate fundamental actions of disjunction and conjunction, separation and union, struggle and reconciliation etc. The movement from one to the other, involving the transfer on the surface of some entity – a quality, an object – from one actant to the other, constitutes the essence of the narrative.

In so far as this sequence can be said to represent an enactment or, as Greimas puts it, 'an extrapolation' of the fundamental structure of syntax (subject–verb–object)[2] it may be thought appropriate to the primal 'dramatic' mode to which Man, as Talking Animal, is

[1] Jameson, *op. cit.*, p. 125.

[2] *Sémantique Structurale*, p. 185.

committed and in whose terms he conceives the world. This, in a
nutshell, is Greimas's case: all narratives exemplify the fundamental
'enunciation spectacle' appropriate to *homo loquens*. And this means that
the semantic structure of sentences will imprint itself on much larger
entities. As Culler says, one of the chief functions of this scheme 'is to
make the structure of the sentence roughly homologous to the "plot"
of a text'.[1]

Like Propp, therefore, Greimas argues for a 'grammar' of narrative in
which a finite number of elements, disposed in a finite number of
ways, will generate the structures that we recognize as stories. But,
unlike Propp, he sees the story as a semantic structure analogous to the
sentence and yielding itself to an appropriate kind of analysis. In pursuit of this aim, he proposes first an inventory of actants (derived in the
main from an amalgam of the work of Propp and another analyst
Souriau), and then three 'actantial categories'; that is, three sets of
binary oppositions, into which all the actants can be fitted, and which
will generate all the actors of any story.[2]

Propp's seven 'spheres of action', it will be remembered, were as
follows:

1   villain
2   donor (provider)
3   helper
4   sought-for person and her father
5   dispatcher
6   hero
7   false hero.

By a reduction or regularization of these into three pairs of opposed
'actants', Greimas aims to emphasize, not the individual items, but the
structural relationship between them. His reorganization produces the
following categories:

　1 Subject versus Object. This subsumes Propp's categories of hero

---

[1] Jonathan Culler, *op. cit.*, p. 82. See also Roger Fowler's extensive argument on this basis
in his *Linguistics and the Novel* ('New Accents', London: Methuen, 1977).
[2] See *Sémantique Structurale*, pp. 175–80.

(Subject) and sought-for person (Object), and characteristically generates stories of quest, or desire.

2 Sender (*Destinateur*) versus Receiver (*Destinataire*). This reveals, says Greimas, the naiveté of some of Propp's categories, for in them the basic *actant* Sender turns out to be articulated in terms of two of its *acteurs*. The first of these (the father) appears in category 4, confused with the object of the quest or desire (the sought-for person), while the second appears in category 5 (the dispatcher). In fact, both are aspects of the single *actant* Sender in a category which characteristically generates stories whose general bearing is that of 'communication'.[1]

These two categories seem fundamental to Greimas, whether they merge in one story involving just two *acteurs*, as in a banal love story where the following structure pertains:

$$\frac{\text{Him}}{\text{Her}} = \frac{\text{Subject and Receiver}}{\text{Object and Sender}}$$

– or in a more complex narrative, such as the Quest for the Holy Grail, where four *acteurs* are involved:

$$\frac{\text{Subject}}{\text{Object}} \quad\quad \frac{\text{Hero}}{\text{Holy Grail}}$$

$$\text{and}$$

$$\frac{\text{Sender}}{\text{Receiver}} \quad\quad \frac{\text{God}}{\text{Man}}^{2}$$

These two categories, it will be noted, offer an enactment of the 'elementary structure' of signification, A:B:: –A: –B, on which our humanity rests, and thus fulfil Greimas's requirement that, in order to have a meaning, a narrative must form a signifying whole and 'thus is organized as an elementary semantic structure' (*Du Sens*, p. 187).

There is a third largely auxiliary category, in which the desire or communication proposed in the other two is helped or hindered.

3 Helper (*Adjuvant*) versus Opponent (*Opposant*). It subsumes Propp's

---

[1] See the discussion, *Sémantique Structurale*, p. 178.

[2] See *Sémantique Structurale*. pp. 177–8.

categories 2 and 3 on the one hand (donor and helper) and 1 (villain) on the other. Presumably Propp's category 7 (false hero) also implies the *opposant* function, though Greimas does not say so.

If these categories of actantial opposition can be said to represent some sort of 'phonemic' level of analysis, then another level of 'syntactic' analysis is also required – one which will try to give an account of the ways in which these elements may be joined together to form narratives – in order that the 'grammar' be complete. Following the lead given by Lévi-Strauss's suggested modification of Propp,[1] Greimas begins by pointing out that Propp's thirty-one 'functions' may also be considerably reduced, if one recognizes their potential for binary 'oppositional' combination or *couplage*.[2] Thus, where Propp lists 'prohibition' and 'violation' as separate functions, Greimas combines them into one: 'prohibition versus violation', on the grounds that the terms presuppose each other: an act of violation requires a prior prohibition in order to define it. Once again, Greimas's insistence on the relationship between entities, rather than the entities themselves, marks him as a structuralist, and his system of semantic analysis reminds us of what might be thought of as the fundamental structuralist obligation: the 'obligation to articulate any apparently static free-standing concept or term into that binary opposition which it structurally presupposes and which forms the very basis for its intelligibility'.[3]

Thus, if we step slightly further back, the 'prohibition-violation' opposition can be seen to be part of a larger pattern of oppositions within Greimas's new 'reduced' inventory of twenty 'functions'. One of these refers to the function whereby the hero is *commanded* or *enjoined* to do something or to go somewhere. Propp calls this a moment of *mediation*, or a *connective incident*, and Greimas reduces this to a relationship between *mandement* (mediation, enjoining, commanding) and *acceptation* (acceptance of the command). If we now recall the model of the 'elementary structure' of signification, A:B:: −A: −B, it will be seen that prohibition acts as the 'negative transformation' of command, just as

---

[1] 'L'analyse morphologique des contes russes', *International Journal of Slavic Linguistics and Poetics*, Vol. 3, 1960, pp. 122–49.

[2] *Sémantique Structurale*, p. 194.

[3] Jameson, *op. cit.*, p. 164.

violation acts as the 'negative transformation' of acceptance on exactly those lines. Seen thus, these four functions can be said to generate a distinctive type of narrative structure which, at the deepest level, speaks of matters of contractual obligation: i.e.,

$$\text{if } \frac{\text{command}}{\text{acceptance}} = \text{establishment of contract}$$

$$\text{then } \frac{\text{prohibition}}{\text{violation}} = \text{breaking of contract}^1$$

Although Greimas makes no attempt at an exhaustive listing, he does, by the means indicated, proceed to isolate various distinctive structures (*syntagmes*) which, he claims, can be discerned in folk narrative:[2]

1 Contractual structures (*syntagmes contractuels*) in which the situation has the overall bearing of the establishing and breaking of contracts, alienation and/or reintegration, etc., as outlined above.
2 Performative structures (*syntagmes performanciels*) involving trials, struggles, the performance of tasks etc.
3 Disjunctive structures (*syntagmes disjonctionnels*) involving movement, departure, arrival etc.

– and so on. It is impossible to give anything like the full details of Greimas's analysis, but enough has been presented to indicate the method by which it proceeds.

He goes on, ultimately, to develop an analysis of the 'semantic system' of the novelist Georges Bernanos which sees his works as articulating from the 'elementary structure of signification' an entire 'univers Bernanosien' whose fundamental symbolic conflict between life and death derives, *via* various 'transformations' from the primary *Axiologie*

$$\frac{\text{Joy}}{\text{Ennui}} - \frac{\text{Disgust}}{\text{Suffering}}^3$$

---

[1] *Sémantique Structurale*, pp. 195–6.

[2] *Du Sens*, p. 191.

[3] *Sémantique Structurale*, p. 256. Cf. Jameson's application of a similar 'elementary structure of signification' to Dickens's *Hard Times* (*op. cit.*, pp. 167 ff.).

In essence, then, Greimas's work in this area constitutes a development and refinement of Propp's original insights, and his ultimate goal is the same as Propp's: the establishment of basic plot 'paradigms', and an exploration of the full range of their combinatory potential: the construction, in other words, of what the structuralists would call a narrational *combinatoire*, or story-generating mechanism: a competence of narrative, which generates the performance of stories; a *langue*, in short, of literature.[1]

TZVETAN TODOROV

With the work of Tzvetan Todorov we shift from an emphasis on literature as writing to an emphasis on the concomitant activity of reading.

Like Greimas, Todorov begins with the notion that there exists, at a deep level, a 'grammar' of narrative from which individual stories ultimately derive. Indeed, there exists a 'universal grammar' which underlies *all* languages. This universal grammar acts as 'the source of all universals and it defines for us even man himself'.[2]

In short, where Whorf, Sapir and others argued that the 'shape' of a culture's language imprinted itself firmly and radically on that culture's experience of the world, Todorov argues for a common human basis of experience which goes beyond the limits of a particular language, and which ultimately informs, not only all languages, but all signifying systems:

> Not only all languages, but also all signifying systems conform to the same grammar. It is universal not only because it informs all the languages of the universe, but because it coincides with the structure of the universe itself.[3]

Of course, language is the primary signifying system among human

---

[1] Greimas's most recent work is *Maupassant: la sémiotique du texte: exercises pratiques* (Paris: Seuil, 1976). On the subject of poetics see his essay 'Pour une théorie du discours poétique' in A. J. Greimas (ed.), *Essais de Sémiotique Poétique* (Paris: Larousse, 1971), pp. 6–24.

[2] Tzvetan Todorov, *Grammaire du Décaméron* (The Hague: Mouton, 1969), p. 15.

[3] *Ibid.*

beings, and its 'grammar' is the determining one, the 'model' for all other systems. So, since art constitutes another signifying system, then 'we can be certain of discovering in it the imprint of the abstract forms of language'.[1] It follows that, as literature is the form of art which derives most closely from language, the study of literature will enjoy a privileged status for *homo loquens*, enabling us to cast new light on the properties of language. Todorov tests this notion by attempting to describe the 'grammar' of Boccaccio's *The Decameron*.

It would be impossible to give a full account of Todorov's 'grammar' here, but its most obvious characteristic is its sophistication of Propp's classifications. Initially, Todorov isolates three dimensions or 'aspects' of the narrative: its *semantic* aspect (i.e. its content); its *syntactical* aspect (its combinations of various structural units); and its *verbal* aspect (its manipulation of the particular words and phrases, 'les phrases con-crètes', in which the story is told).[2] Where Greimas's concern was mainly with semantics, Todorov's is centred almost wholly upon syntax. His analysis of the syntax of the stories of *The Decameron* reveals two fundamental units of structure: *propositions* and *sequences*.

Propositions are the basic elements of syntax. They consist of 'irreducible' actions which act as the fundamental units of the narrative: e.g. 'X makes love to Y'. In practice such a unit may appear as a series of related propositions, e.g. 'X decides to leave home'; 'X arrives at Y's house' and so on (*Grammaire du Décaméron* pp. 19–20).

A *sequence* is a related collection or string ('une certaine suite') of propositions capable of constituting a complete and independent story. A story may contain many sequences: it must contain at least one (*Grammaire du Décaméron* p. 20).

Todorov then proceeds to 'x-ray' the stories of *The Decameron* in these terms, using the model suggested by grammar: that is, the units which make up propositions and sequences are treated as *parts of speech*, while the propositions and sequences themselves function as 'sentences' and 'paragraphs' which make up the whole of the *récit* or text. In this way,

[1] Todorov, 'Language and literature' in Richard Macksey and Eugenio Donato, eds., *The Structuralist Controversy*, p. 125.

[2] *Grammaire du Décaméron*, p. 18. Robert Scholes's account of Todorov's work (*Structuralism in Literature: an Introduction*, pp. 111–17) is extremely helpful, and I have drawn upon it in what follows.

characters can be seen as *nouns*, their 'attributes' as *adjectives* and their actions as *verbs*. 'Rules' can then be discerned which, operating on the model of the rules of syntax in language, govern the formation of propositions and sequences. In general terms, the whole text is seen, as it is by Greimas, as a kind of sentence-structure writ large.

Thus, propositions are formed by the combination of a noun (*character*) with either an adjective (*attribute*) or a verb (*action*). In *The Decameron* each *character* is wholly defined by the combination with attribute or action (*op. cit.* pp. 27–30). All *attributes* are reducible to three 'adjectival' categories: states (*états*), interior properties (*propriétés*) and exterior conditions (*statuts*) (*op. cit.* pp. 30–4). All *actions* are reducible to three 'verbs': 'to modify a situation'; 'to transgress'; and 'to punish' (*op. cit.* pp. 34–41). As a result, all propositions are committed to one of five *modes*: the indicative mode (*mode indicatif*); the obligatory and the optative modes (*modes de la volonté*); and the conditional and the predictive modes (*modes de l'hypothèse*) (*op. cit.* pp. 46–8).

There are three types of relation between propositions which characterize *sequences*: temporal relations, involving simple succession of time; logical relations which deal in cause and effect; and spatial relations, involving parallelism with multiple subdivisions (*op. cit.* pp. 19–20; 53–60). These relations determine the structure of the sequences which may then be classified as either (*a*) *Attributive*, i.e. stories which concern themselves largely with the presentation of characters (*histories d'attribut*) or (*b*) *Retributive*, i.e. stories involving 'séquences de lois', largely concerned with laws, the breaking of laws, and the punishment of lawbreakers (*histoires de punition*) (*op. cit.*, pp. 60–4).

Finally, *The Decameron* manifests ambiguity at the level of both proposition (*ambiguité propositionelle*) and of sequence (*ambiguité sequentielle*) (*op. cit.* pp. 64–8) as well as various types of combination of sequences such as sequence A plus sequence B (*enchaînement*); A plus B plus A (*enchâssement*); or A plus B plus A plus B (*alternance*) (*op. cit.* pp. 68–71).

It must be remembered that Todorov is offering a 'grammar' on the level of *syntax* only: its apparently 'sterile' nature comes precisely from its lack of concern with 'content'. In this, it has obvious parallels with the grammars of languages proposed by structural linguists, in which the question of 'meaning' had no immediate interest for the grammarian, and where the greatest crime was held to be that of 'mixing levels':

of using the 'level' of meaning as the justification for a language's behaviour on the quite different level of its structure.

On the other hand, Todorov's analysis does gesture in the direction of a world beyond itself, which has had its shaping effect; the 'real' world of history and economics:

> If the book has a general sense, it is certainly that of a liberation in exchange – of a break with the old system in the name of audacious personal initiative. In this sense, it would be quite reasonable to say that Boccaccio is a defender of free enterprise and even, if you wish, of nascent capitalism . . .
>
> (*Grammaire du Décaméron*, p. 81)

The vagueness of such statements may be irritating, but they do indicate valuable areas for future research into the relationship between narrative forms and historical exigencies.

Todorov's 'grammar' of *The Decameron* is finally much more complex than is suggested here and it yields a system of notation by whose means the 'structure' of any particular story in the collection may be recorded. It has one major advantage and one major disadvantage.

The disadvantage is obviously its complexity, deriving from its inevitable emphasis on particular performance, rather than general competence; on *The Decameron* itself rather than on the 'rules of the game' which produced those stories, although this is certainly the analyst's ultimate quarry. The advantage must lie in the extent to which such analysis loosens the anaesthetic grip that fiction has on us, as members of a society committed for so long to 'literary' modes of perception. It forces us to look again at stories, and to recognize them for what they are: particular uses of language, or rather of that derivative of language, writing. The analysis of stories in the linguistic 'grammatical' mode proposed by Todorov, pushes their linguistic nature into the foreground for the moment. And this has an effect well described by Fredric Jameson:

> The most characteristic feature of Structuralist criticism lies precisely in a kind of transformation of form into content, in which the form of Structuralist research (stories are organized like sentences, like

linguistic enunciations) turns into a proposition about content: literary works are about language, take the process of speech itself as their essential subject matter.

(The Prison-House of Language, pp. 198–9)

The notion that literary works are ultimately *about* language, that their medium is their message, is one of the most fruitful of structuralist ideas and we have already noticed its theoretical foundation in the work of Jakobson. It validates the post-romantic sense that form and content are one, because it postulates that form *is* content. At one level, this permits, for instance, Todorov to argue that the ultimate *subject* of a work like *The Thousand and One Nights* is the act of story-telling, of narration itself: that for the characters involved – indeed for *homo loquens* at large – 'narration equals life: the absence of narration death',[1] just as it permits a similar argument in respect of the oral art of drama to be made for the plays of Shakespeare.[2] In fact, it finally permits Todorov to postulate, like Jakobson, that all literary works are ultimately self-reflexive; about themselves:

Every work, every novel, tells through its fabric of events the story of its own creation, its own history . . . the meaning of a work lies in its telling itself, its speaking of its own existence.[3]

At another level, this notion finally validates Todorov's own sense (shared by Jakobson) that the study of literature will eventually serve to illuminate the study of language.

If the structuralist approach to literature pushes its privileged 'linguistic' dimension into the foreground, it also raises two other connected matters: the relation of pieces of writing to other pieces of writing (i.e. the question of *genre*) and the question of the relation of a piece of writing to the nature of the act which it presupposes, and which 'completes' it: the act of reading.

---

[1] *Grammaire du Décaméron*, p. 92. Todorov uses *récit* here in the sense of 'narration'. See the whole section, 'Les hommes-récits', pp. 85–97.

[2] See Terence Hawkes, *Shakespeare's Talking Animals* (London: Edward Arnold, 1973), *passim*.

[3] *Littérature et signification*, p. 49. Cf. Jameson's discussion of this notion, *op. cit.*, pp. 200–1.

Todorov treats the question of genre in his *Introduction à la littérature fantastique*. His fundamental argument claims that a 'grammar' of literary forms is as necessary as a 'grammar' of narrative itself. All writing takes place in the light of other writing, and represents a response to the 'world' of writing that pre-exists and therefore stands as the *langue* to its *parole*. However, unlike other structures, the literary structure permits the *parole* to modify the *langue*. As Todorov points out, the literary genre is not like the empirically observed generic 'class' of a science. Each new novel is not only generated by the pre-existing notion of what a novel is, but it can also *change* that notion, and so itself generate a modified one. The genre is therefore not altogether a *prescriptive* concept.

Nevertheless, a world without a theory of *genre* is unthinkable, and untrue to experience. We can tell the difference between a comedy and a tragedy, even if those terms are not as precise and as exclusive as we might wish them to be. Without such a theory, as Todorov says, 'we remain the prisoners of prejudices transmitted from century to century'. The distinction between the theoretical genre and the 'historical' or actual one, i.e. the one that emerges from the 'fact' of what is written, is therefore dynamic, each having its effect on the other. The definition of genres, Todorov concludes, cannot be fixed: it 'is therefore a continual coming and going between the description of facts and the abstraction of theory'.[1]

For instance, Todorov offers an account of the *genre* of the 'fantastic' (*le fantastique*) which describes it as bounded by the neighbouring genres of the uncanny (*l'étrange*) and the marvellous (*le merveilleux*) but never straying into either region, however much it may be drawn in one direction or the other, and indeed however much it may *embody* the tension that such a state creates.[2] Thus the *fantastic* essentially manifests itself in ambiguity, in the hesitation felt by someone who knows only natural laws, when faced with an event which is apparently supernatural. Moreover, the reader, integrated by the genre into the world

[1] *Introduction à la littérature fantastique*, p. 26. See the discussion of genre by Scholes, *op. cit.*, pp. 128–41.

[2] Todorov, 'The fantastic in fiction', trans. Vivienne Mylne, in *Twentieth Century Studies*, Vol. 3, May 1970, pp. 76–92.

of the characters, receives only that information which makes him participate in the ambiguous nature of the situation. As a result, he shares the protagonists' hesitation when it comes to assigning events to the real world or the world of the supernatural.

Thus the genre of the fantastic implies not only the narration of a strange event, but also *a certain way of reading* it: one which will not commit itself either to an allegorical reading of the events, or to any other mode (e.g. the 'poetical') that would 'normalize' and so dispose of them. So the hesitation between natural and supernatural which the narration of the story requires, must be repeated in the responses of the *character* the narration describes, and then echoed in the reader's own hesitation over the culturally available alternatives for his response. At the end of the story the reader (but not the protagonist) is able to resolve his hesitation by opting to classify the events of the story in one or other of the neighbouring areas, the uncanny or the marvellous, depending on the way in which he feels matters have been resolved, and according to a 'scale' that Todorov ingeniously calibrates as follows:

pure uncanny	fantastic-uncanny	fantastic-marvellous	pure marvellous

Ultimately, Todorov argues, the role of the fantastic has always been to set that which is 'real' (i.e. capable of natural explanation) against that which is imaginary or supernatural. Hence it can only exist as a genre in a society which articulates its own experience in terms of that simple dichotomy. In setting the terms of the dichotomy in doubt (are these events real or are they imaginary? How can we be sure?) the literature of the fantastic may indeed have the role of 'the uneasy conscience of the positivist nineteenth century' – the period in which the genre flourished. It suggests, in short, to that society, that life is not as simple as it collectively makes out. And it follows that, in a period like our own, which does not view the world in such simplistic terms, its existence will be more difficult to establish and maintain. We no longer believe in an external, objective, unchanging 'reality', nor in methods which seek merely to transcribe it. For us, the concept of what is 'natural' has been considerably stretched, so that we no longer believe in an 'imaginary', supernatural world clearly opposed to the 'real' one either. For us, 'real' and 'imaginary' are not mutually exclusive categories: they partake of each other. In other words, we no longer believe in the one orthodoxy that the genre of the fantastic exists to challenge: its job is done.

Of course one of the most significant features of the nature of literature is the fact that the concept of genre is as useful to the consumer as to the producer. In fact, as Jonathan Culler points out, the concept of genre offers a 'norm or expectation to guide the reader in his encounter with the text'.[1] A genre-word, 'novel', 'poem', 'tragedy' placed on the cover of a book 'programmes' our reading of it, reduces its complexity, or rather gives it a knowable shape, enabling us literally to 'read' it, by giving it a context and a framework which allows order and complexity to appear. As Culler points out, we know that comedy and tragedy exist, not because of any material difference in *content* – the events of numerous fictions could fall into either (or both) categories – but because they demand different *readings* – from us, and are 'programmed' to demand such readings and to yield themselves accordingly. 'Comedy exists by virtue of the fact that to read something as a comedy involves different expectations from reading something as a tragedy . . .'[2]

In short, to be successful, a theory of genres would have to give an account of those elements of pre-supposition and expectation whose role in the process of reading and writing enabled the reader to *decode* literature in the same mode as it was *encoded* by the writer. Perhaps 'decode' is a misleading term here, for it suggests that there exists an ultimately 'uncoded' message. This is not the case, for as we have seen in the work of Whorf, Sapir and Lévi-Strauss, all our experience is 'coded' for us ultimately by our total way of life. A better term would be 're-code', by which is meant the activity of reducing or 'trimming' all experience to make it fit the categories we have ready for it.

Genres are the literary aspect of these categories. Their boundaries are the boundaries of what Culler calls the 'possibilities of meaning'[3] of a

---

[1] Jonathan Culler, *Structuralist Poetics*, p. 136.

[2] *Op. cit.*, p. 137.

[3] *Op. cit.*, p. 137.

text. And as Todorov's example of the genre of the 'fantastic' shows, each one can exist only when the society's presuppositions, its culture, has a place for it. Genres, then, are essentially culture-bound, 'relative' phenomena. To define genre in this way has the effect of distributing emphasis more equally between the complementary acts of writing, and of reading. As a result, reading becomes an aspect of the total process by which we 'enculturate' all our experience, make it 'natural' and perceptible; make it *capable* of being experienced; make it, in short, *exist*.

Todorov's account of reading in *Poétique de la Prose* represents an attempt to give prominence to an activity we tend to ignore. He points out that one of the main reasons for this is that prevailing critical orthodoxies either look *through* the text to something beyond it: the author, or 'society'; or they seek to *explicate* it by a process of commentary whose final term would be paraphrase – an evident circularity. In place of these he recommends an approach to prose whose quarry is its *poetics*: that is, the general principles which individual works embody in themselves.

The approach which combines close concern for the individual work with a larger awareness of the machinery of its *poetics* is what Todorov terms *reading*. Reading sees the individual work as an autonomous system, but it eschews the 'sticking-to-the-text' aspect which limits mere explication, because it is permanently aware of the text's status as a system and of its relation to a larger system. 'Literary theory (poetics) provides criticism with instruments; yet criticism does not content itself with applying them in a servile fashion, but transforms them through the contact with new material.'[1]

Hence the reader will not look for 'hidden' meanings, and give them preference, as in the activity of *interpretation*; he will be concerned with the relationship between the various *levels* of meaning, with the multiplicity which the text, as a system, enjoys. He will perform operations such as 'superposition' and 'figuration' which see a text or group of texts as obedient to the nature of a certain 'figure' or structure which can be discerned in various modes and at various levels, so that a novel

[1] Todorov, 'The structural analysis of literature: the tales of Henry James' in David Robey, ed., *Structuralism, an Introduction*, p. 73.

may in its plot and characterization enact the dominant 'shape' of a particular figure of speech, or pattern of syntax. Such reading looks for the 'figure in the carpet' beyond the overt content, and is well exemplified in Todorov's own reading of Henry James's short stories, where James, it is argued, 'erects his method as a narrator into a philosophical concept' so that the stories repeatedly evince 'an essential secret' which itself gives rise to their essential organizing structure 'based on the quest for an absolute and absent cause'. The secret turns out to be the the existence of a secret, and the 'figure in the carpet' manifests a number of variations at a variety of levels, while never losing its unifying identity. In short, the question of a 'right' reading never arises. The critic concerns himself with what Scholes calls 'readings that are more or less rich, strategies that are more or less appropriate'.[1]

This means that:

1 Each literary text contains a potentiality for transforming the whole system that it embodies and that has produced it: it does not merely rehearse preordained categories and combine them in novel ways. On the contrary, it modifies what it consists of.

2 The literary text is able to subvert the linguistic system it inherits: it does not merely exhibit the characteristic forms of the language which contains it, it also extends and modifies that language. After all, writing, the raw material of reading, is not the same thing as language. Thus 'literature is, inside language, what destroys the metaphysics inherent in every language. The essence of literary discourse is to go beyond language (if not, it would have no *raison d'être*): literature is like a deadly weapon with which language commits suicide'.[2]

It follows that:

3 The literary text is *totally* significant and signifying, and cannot be 'reduced' to our articulation of its 'content'. Writing communicates in ways in which language does not – e.g. in its ordering of events through linear progression – and these need to be taken into account. Writing does not simply *contain*.[3]

---

[1] Scholes, *op. cit.*, p. 145.
[2] 'The fantastic in fiction', *op. cit.*, p. 91.
[3] Cf. *Poétique de la prose* pp. 246–7.

These ideas concerning the activity of reading perhaps represent Todorov's most seminal contribution to the structuralist view of literature. They are fully taken up by Roland Barthes, whose analysis of the special nature of writing and reading has proved central to the development of structuralist literary criticism.

ROLAND BARTHES

The term 'codes' has already been used and it is appropriate now to explore its implications a little further. The notion that we 'encode' our experience of the world in order that we *may* experience it; that there exists, in general, no pristine range of experiences open to us, comes directly, as we have seen, from the work of Sapir, Whorf and Lévi-Strauss.

We thus invent the world we inhabit: we modify and reconstruct what is given. It follows that, implicated as we all are in this gigantic, covert, collaborative enterprise, none of us can claim access to uncoded, 'pure' or *objective* experience of a 'real', permanently existing world. None of us, in short, is innocent. It is necessary to raise these rather general matters again, however briefly, before discussing the work of Roland Barthes precisely because the totality of his work may most fruitfully be seen as an attack on the *presumption* of innocence: something which Barthes sees as a characteristic corruption of modern bourgeois society.

The attack began in his first book, *Le Degré Zéro de l'Écriture* (1953) (translated as *Writing Degree Zero*). Here Barthes focuses attention on the classical French style of writing (*écriture classique*) as a phenomenon which, established on a national scale in the mid-seventeenth century, encounters a crisis of confidence in the mid-nineteenth century.

Not until then, he argues, did it become possible to discern that such *écriture* was in fact a style at all: a particular, deliberately adopted 'way' of writing developed at a particular time and place. For the practitioners of the style had hitherto inculcated a sense of its inevitability; a sense that such a way of writing was the only right or rational one. An innocent reflection of reality, universally suitable for all times and places, it seemed not really a style so much as the nature of writing itself. Barthes sees this process as a characteristic act of bourgeois expropriation, part of a grand design whereby all aspects of bourgeois life silently acquire the same air of naturalness, of rightness, of universality and inevitability. But bourgeois *écriture* is not innocent. It does not simply reflect reality. In fact, it *shapes* reality in its own image, acting as the institutionalized carrier, transmitter or encoder of the bourgeois way of life and its values. To respond to such writing is to accede to those values, to confirm and to reinforce the nature of that way of life. When that way of life disintegrates, as it began to do in the mid-nineteenth century, then the style that supported it, and that it supported, will disintegrate also, and writers will either seek for a different style or, recognizing the style *as* a style for the first time, will seek to abandon style altogether.

Hence, since 1850, the stylistic phenomena recognized by literary historians: the multiplication of various styles; the concept of style as a painstakingly acquired 'craftmanship' (e.g. in Flaubert), the self-consciousness about style, often resulting in a conglomerate style which draws on, or scores off, others (e.g. Joyce, Eliot) and the various efforts towards a 'zero degree' of style, a 'style-less', blank, transparent way of writing (e.g. Camus, Hemingway). Of course, a style-less or 'colourless' way of writing ultimately proves impossible to achieve, since it quickly becomes a noticeable style in itself. Hemingway's pugnaciously non-literary manner is nothing if not distinctive, and so-called 'realistic' writing like Zola's, 'far from being neutral . . . is on the contrary loaded with the most spectacular signs of fabrication'.[1]

Barthes's major premiss as a structuralist critic is that writing is *all* style, that 'white writing' does not and cannot exist; 'writing is in no way an instrument for communication, it is not an open route through which there passes only the intention to speak.'[2] Nor do any trans-historical, universal stylistic modes or conditions such as 'precision' or 'clarity' exist in contexts that are innocent of ideology: 'In actual fact, clarity is a purely rhetorical attribute, not a quality of language in general which is possible at all times and in all places.'[3] Indeed, Barthes would add, the notion that such things are *intrinsic* qualities of a

---

[1] *Writing Degree Zero*, p. 74.
[2] *Ibid.*, p. 25.
[3] *Ibid.*, p. 64.

certain kind of writing, and not features *extrinsically* determined in the light of economic and political conditions, is an elaborate pretence. It reveals the definitive historical commitment of an aggressive bourgeoisie, anxious to reduce all human experience to fit the shape of its own particular view of the world, which it promotes as 'natural' and 'normal', refusing to recognize what it cannot so classify.[1]

In place of this deceitful process, Barthes offers the notion of literature as what Fredric Jameson calls a highly 'conventionalized activity'.[2] In it, the Saussurean signifier–signified relationship is complicated by 'another type of signification which bears on the nature of the code itself.' In consequence, literature exhibits a fundamental duplicity: it offers a *meaning*, and at the same time 'wears a label' to which it points. In Jameson's words, 'each literary work, above and beyond its own determinate content, also signifies literature in general . . . identifies itself for us as a literary product'. That is, it announces that we are in the presence of 'literariness' and so 'involves us in that particular and historical social activity which is the consumption of literature'.[3]

This can be done through its 'tone', its use of particular items of vocabulary, its use, in the nineteenth-century novel, of particular stylistic devices such as the 'narrative third person' or the preterite tense:

> Obsolete in spoken French, the preterite, which is the cornerstone of Narration, always signifies the presence of Art; it is part of a ritual of Letters. Its function is no longer that of a tense . . . it is the ideal instrument for every construction of a world . . . Thanks to it, reality is neither mysterious nor absurd; it is clear, almost familiar . . .[4]

These literary signs also act as indicators of social class, signalling – indeed offering – membership of the bourgeoisie through their projection of the bourgeois world-view, and their presumption that such a world-view is acceptable to that exclusive group of consumers who (in

---

[1] *Writing Degree Zero*, pp. 61–7.
[2] Jameson, *op. cit.*, p. 154.
[3] Jameson, *op. cit.*, p. 155.
[4] *Ibid.*, pp. 36–7.

a consumer-based society) 'consume' literature. This results in a paradox to which bourgeois literary criticism is traditionally and systematically blind. As Jameson puts it, 'At the same time that (literature) poses its own universality, the very words it uses to do so signal their complicity with that which makes universality unrealizable.'[1]

The transaction between writer and reader that 'literature' involves can thus be said to be the opposite of innocent. In fact, it emerges as a complex social, political, even economic affair and Barthes's later theory has developed the notion that the process involves a no less complex – even ornate – structure of codes. The codes act as agencies – whether we are conscious of them or not – which *modify, determine* and, most importantly, *generate* meaning in a manner far from innocent, far from untrammelled, and very much closer to the complicated ways in which language itself imposes its own mediating, shaping pattern on what we like to think of as an objective world 'out there'. As a result, any text will reveal, when properly analysed, not a simple reflection of reality, but the sort of *multiplicity* which Todorov recognizes as distinctive.

Possibly the best-known application of these ideas in early form occurs in Barthes's collection of demystifying essays, *Mythologies* (1957, 1970) where a remorseless analysis of the 'myths' generated by French mass media lays bare their covert manipulation of the codes for their own purposes. Despite the overt stance of the media, that no such codes exist, that they innocently present the real world as it actually is, Barthes's analysis subtly and amusingly reveals a contrary aim: the generation, confirmation and reinforcement of a particular view of the world in which bourgeois values emerge, as usual, as inevitable and 'right' at all levels, whether in respect of the role of the writer in society, the size of Einstein's brain, or the nature and function of detergents: 'Products based on chlorine and ammonia are without doubt the representatives of a kind of absolute fire, a saviour but a blind one. Powders, on the contrary, are selective, they push, they drive dirt through the texture of the object, their function is keeping public order not making war.'[2]

[1] *Op. cit.*, p. 158.

[2] *Mythologies*, p. 36. The theoretical conclusions of Barthes's analysis in *Mythologies* make an important contribution to the theory of semiotics, and are discussed below, pp. 106–9.

A later instance of the critical application of the same method to one of the pillars of what Barthes has called 'this awe-inspiring mystery: French literature' occurs in his *Sur Racine* (1963) in which Racine's plays appear, not as the polished vehicles for a moral view of the world as approved by the French literary establishment, but as the basis of a 'Racinian anthropology' whose complex, highly patterned system of thematic 'oppositions', generates a variety of hitherto unheard-of (or suppressed) pyschological structures. Such outrageous 'desecration', undertaken in the name of literary criticism, provoked the scandalized pamphlet of Professor Raymond Picard, *Nouvelle critique ou nouvelle imposture* (1965), to which Barthes replied in his *Critique et vérité* (1966), making the point that while Picard's own criticism naturally claims to be 'innocent', in fact it betrays a commitment to a particular, positivist, bourgeois ideology. As an alternative, and in his own defence, Barthes proclaims the virtues of a criticism which sets out to free itself from such restrictions by means of its espousal of literature's inherent 'plurality', its embracing of the literary text as, in Todorov's terms, *totally* significant and signifying, its commitment to ambiguity, its refusal to give itself to a single vision, and its ultimate status as a 'critique' of language.

The notions that plurality and ambiguity can be seen as virtues, not vices of literature, and that a deliberately invoked tension between meanings can reveal a good deal about the nature of language, are perhaps not unfamiliar to English or American students of the subject who have been exposed to the ideas of Richards, Empson, Leavis and others. But Barthes's 'outlaw' status confirms that they have tended to order these things differently in France.

In fact, Barthes's notions have an American flavour. Just as Whorf and Sapir argue that the so-called objective world does not exist 'out there', but is manufactured by us within and through our total pattern of behaviour, so Barthes insists that literature has no single 'natural' or 'objective' standing beyond our own culture. Literature owes its existence to the codes that we invent to process the world and to create it. It may be a distillation of those codes: that, in a sense, offers an excellent reason for inventing it. It *reminds* the reader of the codes, and shows him how they work. Its 'critique' of language consists in this.

The concept of literature's 'self-contained' nature, its standing as a 'structure' deriving from an interplay of codes, finds confirmation in Barthes's fundamental distinction between two sorts of writer and of writing. We tend, mistakenly, he argues, to think of writing as instrumental, as a vehicle for an ulterior purpose, as a means to action or as the 'dress' of language. Barthes points out that, although writing can serve this purpose, it has acquired over the years another role. There do indeed exist writers who write *about* other things, and for whom the activity of writing is transitive, leading *to* other things. But there also exists the writer for whom the verb 'to write' is *intransitive*; whose central concern is not to take us 'through' his writing to a world beyond it, but to produce Writing. He is an *author*: what Barthes terms an *écrivain*. Unlike the writer (*scripteur écrivant*), who writes for an ulterior purpose in a *transitive* mode, and who intends us to move from his writing to the world beyond it, the *écrivain* has as his field 'nothing but writing itself, not as the pure "form" conceived by an aesthetic of art for art's sake but, much more radically, as the only area for the one who writes.'[1] Barthes is here clearly drawing to a certain extent on the principles of Russian Formalism, and in particular on the distinction made by Jakobson, between the 'referential' and the 'aesthetic' functions of language, assigning the former to the *writer*, the latter to the *author*. Where the writer writes *something*, he continues, the author just *writes*, that is all. He aims not to take us *beyond* his writing, but to draw our attention to the activity itself. This constitutes, in one sense, a tautology in that the raw material of the writer thereby becomes the end product of his writing, but it is not unproductive. Barthes's argument moves, in the end, to embrace the full formalist position. Painters paint: they require us to look at their use of colour, form, texture, not to look 'through' their painting at something beyond it. By the same token, musicians present us with sounds, not arguments or events. So, writers write; they offer us *writing* as their art; not as a vehicle, but as an end in itself.

Of course, since writers use words, their art must in the end – as Jakobson points out – be composed of signifiers without signifieds. So it becomes essential that in order to appreciate the work of the *écrivain* our attention should dwell on the signifiers and we should not yield to

[1] Roland Barthes, 'To write: an intransitive verb?' in Macksey and Donato, eds, *The Structuralist Controversy*, p. 144.

our natural urge to move beyond them to the signifieds which they imply. Much modern writing (e.g. Proust, Joyce, Becket) is clearly in this mode, taking the activity of writing as its subject, and obviously trying, by experimental methods, to establish a new 'writerly' status for the writer. Such writing requires a new notion of the concomitant activity of *reading*.

Like Todorov, Barthes could ultimately be said to centre his interest on the reader and the act of reading, and it is in this area that he makes his truly original contribution to the discussion which, as we have seen, has its roots in the work of Saussure, the Russian formalists, Jakobson and others. He even proposes a new taxonomy of literature on this basis. In his critical *tour de force*, S/Z (1970), he argues that literature may be divided into that which gives the reader a role, a function, a contribution to make, and that which renders the reader idle or redundant, 'left with no more than the poor freedom either to accept or reject the text'[1] and which thereby reduces him to that apt but impotent symbol of the bourgeois world, an inert *consumer* to the author's role as producer.

Literature of the second kind, which can only be read in the sense of being 'submitted to', he terms *readerly* (*lisible*). In it, the passage from signifier to signified is clear, well-worn, established and compulsory. Literature of the first kind, which invites us self-consciously to read it, to 'join in' and be aware of the interrelationship of the writing and reading, and which accordingly offers us the joys of co-operation, co-authorship (and even, at its intensest moments, of copulation), he calls *writerly* (*scriptible*). In that sort of writing (it is the sort that attracted the attention and praise of the Russian formalists: we have already noted their admiration of Sterne), the signifiers have free play; no automatic reference to signifieds is encouraged or required.

Where *readerly* texts (usually classics) are static, virtually 'read themselves' and thus perpetuate an 'established' view of reality and an 'establishment' scheme of values, frozen in time, yet serving still as an out-of-date model for our world, *writerly* texts require us to look at the nature of language itself, not *through* it at a preordained 'real world'.

[1] Roland Barthes, S/Z, translated by Richard Miller, p. 4. All references are to this translation.

They thus involve us in the dangerous, exhilarating activity of creating our world *now*, together with the author, as we go along. Where *readerly* texts presuppose and depend upon the presumptions of innocence outlined above, and with them the unquestioned relationship between signifier and signified that those presumptions reinforce, saying 'this is what the world is like and always will be like', *writerly* texts presume nothing, admit no easy passage from signifier to signified, are open to the 'play' of the codes that we use to determine them. In readerly texts the signifiers march: in writerly texts they dance. And paradoxically, where readerly texts (which require no *real* reading) are often what we call 'readable', writerly texts (which demand strenuous reading) are often called 'unreadable'.

The experience offered by the reading of writerly texts has been described by Barthes in his book *Le Plaisir Du Texte* (1975).[1] It involves two kinds of 'pleasure': *plaisir* (pleasure) and *jouissance* (bliss, ecstasy, even sexual delight). *Plaisir* seems to come from the more straightforward processes of reading, *jouissance* from a sense of breakdown or interruption: 'Is not the most erotic portion of a body *where the garment gapes?* . . . it is intermittence, as psychoanalysis has so rightly stated, which is erotic: the intermittence of skin flashing between two articles of clothing . . .'[2] Translated into literary terms this suggests that where pleasure inheres in the overt linguistic ordering imposed by the 'readerly' text on its material, bliss comes about in 'writerly' texts, or at climactic moments in 'readerly' ones, when that order breaks down, when the 'garment gapes', when overt linguistic purpose is suddenly subverted, and so 'orgasmically' transcended:

> Text of pleasure: the text that contents, fills, grants euphoria; the text that comes from culture and does not break with it, is linked to a *comfortable* practice of reading. Text of bliss: the text that imposes a state of loss, the text that discomforts (perhaps to the point of a certain boredom), unsettles the reader's historical, cultural, psychological assumptions, the consistency of his tastes, values, memories, brings to a crisis his relation with language.[3]

[1] Translated by Richard Miller as *The Pleasure of the Text*.

[2] *The Pleasure of the Text*, pp. 9–10.

[3] *Ibid.*, p. 14.

Our creative responses to these latter texts or moments is what turns us into ecstatic *écrivains* as we read.

Possibly the best way to an understanding of these matters is through a consideration of Barthes's analysis of the nature of the codes involved in reading and writing, and of their potential for ecstasy. For this, we must turn to S/Z.[1]

S/Z is the record of Barthes's almost literally shattering analysis of *Sarrasine*, a 'readerly' short story by the arch-realist French writer Balzac. Barthes's aim is to demonstrate the text's *totally* signifying nature. His method is to divide the story (or, in his words, to 'separate' it 'in the manner of a minor earthquake', p. 13) into 561 *lexias* (reading-units of considerably varying length) and then to analyse these 'textual signifiers' in terms of five codes, as follows:

1 The hermeneutic code

This consists of 'all the units whose function it is to articulate in various ways a question, its response, and the variety of chance events which can either formulate the question or delay its answer; or even, constitute an enigma and lead to its solution' (p. 17). This is really the 'story-telling' code, by means of which the narrative raises questions, creates suspense and mystery, before resolving these as it proceeds along its course. Thus, the title of Balzac's story offers a good example of the hermeneutic code (it forces us to ask who?, what? immediately), and the same code can be found in operation in *lexias* such as 'Unfortunately, however, the mystery of the Lantys presented a continuing source of curiosity . . .' which shows the 'coding' of a mystery to which the reader naturally wants a solution, and which the story obviously promises him. This code usually involves syntactic ordering, vocabulary etc., and can be recognized by its general 'shape': a process of mystifying together with the implicit promise of subsequent demystification: the generation of suspense, to be followed by disclosure.

[1] For an excellent account of the full range of Barthes's work, and a particularly good exposition of the meaning of some of his more complex terms, I have found John Sturrock's article 'Roland Barthes; a profile', *The New Review*, Vol. I, No. 2, May 1974, pp. 13–21, very valuable.

2 The code of semes or signifiers

This is a code of connotations which utilizes hints or 'flickers of meaning' (p. 19) generated by certain signifiers: e.g. again in the title of the
story, *Sarrasine*, the final 'e' of the name suggests femininity in this code
– a quality much at the centre of the story's later complications – by a
simple lexical hint or flicker. Lexia (4): 'Midnight had just sounded
from the clock of the Elysée-Bourbon' manifests, in this code, an
encoded 'flicker' concerning ill-gotten wealth for, as Barthes says 'a
neighbourhood of *nouveaux riches*, the Faubourg Saint-Honoré refers by
synecdoche to the Paris of the Bourbon Restoration, a mythic place of
sudden fortunes whose origins are suspect: where gold is produced
without an origin, diabolically (the symbolic definition of specula-
tion)' (p. 21). This code deals to a certain extent in what Anglo-
American criticism familiarly thinks of as 'themes' or 'thematic
structures'.

3 The symbolic code

This is the code of recognizable 'groupings' or configurations, regularly repeated in various modes and by various means in the text,
which ultimately generates the dominant figure in the carpet. Thus, the
lexia (2) 'I was deep in one of those daydreams . . .' offers, in the
'contrary' or 'antithetical' nature of 'day/dream' the first instance of
what will grow into a vast central pattern of antitheses which the story
continuously generates, building up to its climax where the sexual
notion of 'antithesis' (male/female) enters the overall meaning of the
text. To Anglo-American eyes, of course, codes 2 and 3 are not easily
distinguished.

4 The proairetic code

This is the code of 'actions' (p. 18). Derived from the concept of
proairesis, 'the ability rationally to determine the result of an action', this
code is also embodied in sequences such as *lexia* (2) 'I was deep in one
of those daydreams', where the state of absorption indicated ('I was
deep in . . .') 'already implies . . . some event which will bring it to an

end' (p. 18) – that is, a subsequent sequence along the lines of '. . . when something happened to change that state'. Barthes's account of this code is notoriously lax, as he claims that since the proairetic sequences are 'never more than the result of an artifice of reading', i.e. we note or 'record' them as we go along, amassing the data provided by the narrative, then their only definitive characteristic is the *name* we give to each one: 'strolling' sequences, 'murder' sequences etc. So, since 'its basis is therefore more empirical than rational', it is useless to try to schematize it further (p. 19).

5 The 'cultural' code (or 'reference' code)

This code manifests itself as a 'gnomic', collective, anonymous and authoritative voice which speaks for and about what it aims to establish as 'accepted' knowledge or wisdom. *Lexia* (2) yet again contains a good example in the phrase 'one of those daydreams', which refers to an established body of what its author takes to be 'common knowledge', made explicit in *lexia* (3) 'which overtake even the shallowest of men, in the midst of the most tumultuous parties'. The assumption that 'everyone knows' what the author means is clearly reinforced, and the code's function lies there: in the authentication by glancing or 'know-ing' reference, of established and authoritative cultural forms. This is the most controversial of the codes, and the least well-grounded, par-ticularly as Barthes makes the initial and damaging admission that 'of course, all codes are cultural' (p. 18) – a statement which, if true, denies this code any specificity.

The exercise Barthes performs on Balzac's short story has in essence the effect of turning a 'readerly' text into a 'writerly' one. The five codes are deployed intensively as disintegrating agents, often, as we have seen, operating in the same *lexias* at the same time. The total effect is to free the text from its 'background', its context, the limitations imposed on its range by the traditions of historical scholarship and criticism. However, the sheer bravura of the method used arouses cer-tain suspicions. Barthes's most outrageous piece of sleight-of-hand lies in a sense in his presentation of the cultural code as simply *one* of a range of five, thereby promoting the others (which could otherwise easily be demoted to the status of mere *aspects* of a general cultural code) as free-wheeling agents, emitting signals of a distracting and disruptive kind, over and above what the story appears to be saying.

Nevertheless (and this is undoubtedly the point of the exercise) the arch-realist of French literature does not emerge unscathed. In fact he turns out to be no 'realist' at all. His narrative affords no transparent 'innocent' window on to a 'reality' that lies 'beyond' the text. Rather, the text reveals itself as closely akin in nature to the method of analysis that has been applied to it: a minefield of concealed 'shaping' devices, a corridor of distorting mirrors, a heavily *stained* glass window which imposes its colours and its shapes definitively on what (if anything) can be glimpsed through it. In fact most of what we see, Barthes seems to say, is inscribed on the glass: we look *at* such a window, not through it: it functions as a message, not a medium, and one not wholly in the control of its author.

Barthes's fundamental undermining of the idea that a text has a unitary meaning injected into it by a unitary author constitutes of course part of a larger attack on the illusions of individualism that ultimately has a political and economic base. The 'single vision', the reduction of the world to one dimension, the notion that human beings are (or should be) separate entities, each metaphorically surrounded by an inviolable area of individuality, within which reside our 'individual' rights, our 'individual' psyche, our 'individual' personality – these must rank as fairly recent, relatively modern notions. They are, it may be argued, the product of two linked forces – protestantism and capitalism – in which the individual's *personal* relationship to God, and his *personal* commitment to acquire and retain money spring from the same impulse.

The twin notions of an author's *individuality* and of his *originality* come from the same source. Where modern (i.e. post-Renaissance) authors tend more and more to think of their writing as an *expression* – even an extension – of their individuality, medieval authors did not. Indeed, the concept of personal 'authorship' (the author's name on the book he has written) has no real standing in the Middle Ages where works, stories, poems, were more likely to be seen as part of a collective enterprise, expressing no individual 'point of view' (the very phrase suggests one man's *single* vision) but a *general* outlook, the product of the culture at large. The concept of *plagiarism* offers a notable instance:

virtually unknown – because hardly to be conceived of – by that 'collective' medieval society, in a modern, individualistic, monocular society, it becomes the literary version of a crime against property: a kind of theft.

In other words, Barthes's objection to the apparently 'innocent' certainties of the connection between signifier and signified stands ultimately as an objection to an 'individualized' bourgeois social order which rests on those certainties, which constructs its 'reality' on that basis, and which accordingly finds itself committed – politically and economically – to its maintenance and reinforcement. Such a social order's literary establishment – its critics – and that establishment's 'raw material' – its texts – become a major tool in this process. The institutionalizing of a particular vision of reality through the institutionalizing of a particular series of 'classic' texts and of appropriate 'interpretations' of them in an educational system which processes all the members of the society, can clearly act as a potent 'normalizing' force. It is this force which S/Z aims to undermine, by showing first that the text (and so all 'realistic' texts) does not offer an accurate picture of an unchangingly 'real' world, and second, that a reading of it is possible which can tear away the veil, reveal the signifier–signified connection as the un-innocent *convention* (however politically bolstered) it is, and offer a sense that reality remains genuinely ours to make and to remake as we please. The pleasure of that making is creative in nature, and perhaps *jouissance* is a good term for it.

Barthes has recently assigned to Japanese culture an ideal status as a way of life in which signifiers have a higher status than signifieds. His *L'Empire des Signes* (1970) applauds the absence of an 'inner' reality prized higher than the outward sign which 'represents' it in that culture, for it releases its members from the duplicity of the Western signifier–signified articulation. But the West, it should be said, has its modes of *jouissance* too. We have already noticed the connection between Lévi-Strauss's notion of the activities of the 'savage' *bricoleur*, and the *modus operandi* of the jazz musician. The role Barthes gives the critic could also be said to rank him with the jazz musician, as an artist whose art derives from 'given' material, 'given' signifiers (a text, a chord-sequence) but which creates, from these, new signifieds, a new reality which is not given, and which surpasses the original in invention and beauty. This art – an art of signifiers, not signifieds, can be said to be truly modern, whether its modernity manifests itself in *jouissance* or *jazz* (and leaving aside the question of a philological or semantic connection between the two terms). It is also truly revolutionary, a term that can with justification be applied to S/Z.

We have already noticed that concern with signifiers on a semantic level forms a central feature of the work of A. J. Greimas, who sees the signifier–signified connection as, in the long run, infinitely regressive in nature. The connection itself is what generates meaning, not any 'real' world beyond it to which it refers:

> Signification is thus nothing but such transposition from one level of language to another, from one language to a different language, and meaning is nothing but the possibility of such *transcoding*.[1]

The notion that meaning arises from the interplay of signs, that the world we inhabit is not one of 'facts' but of signs *about* facts which we encode and decode ceaselessly from system to system also stands, of course, as a central theme of S/Z. It derives from Barthes's earlier interests in the pervasiveness of coding in all human affairs (e.g. food, clothing)[2] and its role as the distinctive human activity. We live in a world, the argument concludes, which has no 'pure', no 'innocent' contexts to offer us: a world of signs *about*, rather than experience *of*. It follows that structuralism's final inclination must be towards a science appropriate to the analysis of such a world.

---

[1] A. J. Greimas, *Du Sens*, p. 13.
[2] See Barthes's 'Eléments de sémiologie' in *Communications*, Vol. 4, 1964, pp. 91–135, published as *Elements of Semiology*, trans. Annette Lavers and Colin Smith, and his *Système de la mode*.

4

A SCIENCE OF SIGNS

A science that studies the life of signs within society is conceivable; it would be a part of social psychology and consequently of general psychology; I shall call it *semiology* (from the Greek *sēmeîon* 'sign'). Semiology would show what constitutes signs, what laws govern them. Since the science does not yet exist, no one can say what it would be; but it has a right to existence, a place staked out in advance. Linguistics is only a part of the general science of semiology; the laws discovered by semiology will be applicable to linguistics, and the latter will circumscribe a well-defined area within the mass of anthropological facts.

(Ferdinand de Saussure, *Course in General Linguistics*, p. 16)

Logic, in its general sense, is, as I believe I have shown, only another name for *semiotic*, the quasi-necessary, or formal doctrine of signs. By describing the doctrine as 'quasi-necessary', or formal, I mean that we observe the characters of such signs as we know, and from such an observation, by a process which I will not object to naming Abstraction, we are led to statements, eminently fallible, and therefore in one sense by no means necessary, as to what *must* be the characters of all signs used by a 'scientific' intelligence, that is to say by an intelligence capable of learning by experience.

(C. S. Peirce, *Collected Papers*, Vol. 2, Para. 227)

The notion of a 'science of signs', conceived independently and (as we have noticed in the case of a number of linguistic concepts) at about the same time by theorists on opposite sides of the Atlantic, has become one of the most fruitful concepts deriving from the general structuralist enterprise of the last two decades, and not easily distinguishable from it. The terms *semiology* and *semiotics* are both used to refer to this science, the only difference between them being that *semiology* is preferred by Europeans, out of deference to Saussure's coinage of the term, and *semiotics* tends to be preferred by English speakers, out of deference to the American Peirce.[1] The field of semiotics is of course enormous, ranging from the study of the communicative behaviour of animals (*zoosemiotics*) to the analysis of such signifying systems as human bodily communication (*kinesics* and *proxemics*), olfactory signs (the 'code of scents'), aesthetic theory, and rhetoric.[2] By and large, its boundaries (if it has any) are coterminous with those of structuralism: the interests of the two spheres are not fundamentally separate and, in the long run, both ought properly to be included within the province of a third, embracing discipline called, simply, *communication*. In such a context, structuralism itself would probably emerge as a method of analysis linking the fields of linguistics, anthropology and semiotics.[3] I shall therefore attempt only the briefest outline of semiotics here before narrowing the discussion to a consideration of some of its implications for the student of literature.

It has already been argued that in human societies, language clearly plays a commanding role and is generally taken to be the predominant means of communication. But it is also clear that human beings communicate by nonverbal means and in ways which must consequently be said to be either non-linguistic (although the *mode* of language remains formative and dominant) or which must have the effect of 'stretching' our concept of language until it includes non-verbal areas. In fact, such 'stretching' is precisely the great achievement of semiotics. 'What semiotics has discovered,' says Julia Kristeva, '. . . is that the *law*

---

[1] See the excellent account by Pierre Guiraud, *Semiology*, pp. 1–4.

[2] See the rather daunting survey by Umberto Eco, *A Theory of Semiotics*, pp. 9–14.

[3] Cf. Barthes's proposal to invert Saussure's hierarchy and to nominate semiotics as part of linguistics, *Elements of Semiology*, p. 11.

governing or, if one prefers, the *major constraint* affecting any social practice lies in the fact that it signifies; i.e., that it is articulated *like* a
language.'[1] In other words, nobody just talks. Every speech-act includes
the transmission of messages through the 'languages' of gesture, pos-
ture, clothing, hairstyle, perfume, accent, social context etc. over and
above, under and beneath, even at cross-purposes with what words
actually *say*. And even when we are not speaking or being spoken to,
messages from other 'languages' crowd in upon us: horns hoot, lights
flash, laws restrain, hoardings proclaim, smells attract or repel, tastes
delight or disgust, even the 'feel' of objects systematically communicates something meaningful to us. Man's role in the world, such a
situation suggests, is quintessentially one of communication. He is, as
Greimas argues, a receiver and sender of messages: he gathers and
disseminates information. In Sapir's words, 'every cultural pattern and
every single act of social behaviour involves communication in either
an explicit or implicit sense'.[2]

Roman Jakobson suggests an approach to this mass of sign-systems
which begins by considering some general principles:

> Every message is made of signs; correspondingly, the science of signs
> termed *semiotic* deals with those general principles which underlie the
> structure of all signs whatever, and with the character of their utiliza-
> tion within messages, as well as with the specifics of the various sign
> systems, and of the diverse messages using those different kinds of
> signs.
>
> ('Language in relation to other communication systems'
> *Selecting Writings* Vol. II, p. 698)

The study of sign systems derives, Jakobson goes on, from an initial
and very ancient perception that a sign has two aspects: 'an immediately perceptible *signans* and an inferable, apprehensible *signatum*' (*Ibid.*,
p. 699). This does not essentially differ from the distinction between
signifier and signified recorded by Saussure: both elements function as

---

[1] Julia Kristeva, 'The system and the speaking subject', *Times Literary Supplement*, 12 October
1973, p. 1249.
[2] *Selected Writings in Language, Culture, and Personality*, p. 104.

aspects of the 'indissoluble unity' of the sign, and the various relationships possible between them form the basis of semiotic structures.

In fact the American founder of semiotics, the philosopher C. S. Peirce (1839–1914), proposed a complex classification of signs precisely in terms of the different relationship each manifested between *signans* and *signatum*, or signifier and signified. In doing so, he argued that he was confronting nothing less than foundations of logic itself.

For in Peirce's view, logic exists independently of both reasoning and fact. Its fundamental principles are not axioms but 'definitions and divisions' (*Collected Papers*, Vol. 3, para. 149) and these derive ultimately from the nature and functions of signs.[1] As a result, logic can be seen as 'the science of the general necessary laws of signs' (*ibid.*, Vol. 2, para. 227). Logic, that is, is the science of signs.

A sign or *representamen* is 'something which stands to somebody for something in some respect or capacity' (*ibid.*, Vol. 2, para. 228): it is 'anything which determines something else (its *interpretant*) to refer to an object to which itself refers (its *object*)' (*ibid.*, Vol. 2, para. 303). A sign thus *stands for* something (its *object*); it stands for something *to* somebody (its *interpretant*); and finally it stands for something to somebody *in some respect* (this respect is called its *ground*). These terms, *representamen, object, interpretant* and *ground* can thus be seen to refer to the means by which the sign signifies; the relationship between them determines the precise nature of the process of *semiosis*.

The relationship, Peirce argues, normally involves the three elements, *representamen* or sign, *object*, and *ground* in three kinds of 'triadic' structures or 'trichotomies' in whose terms the fourth element, the *interpretant*, perceives. These are

(a) 'triadic relations of comparison' or logical possibilities based on the kind of *sign*. These are the *qualisign*, a 'quality' which acts as a sign once it is embodied; the *sinsign*, an actual thing or event which

---

[1] References are to C. S. Peirce's *Collected Papers* (8 vols.), ed. Charles Hartshorne, Paul Weiss and Arthur W. Burks (Cambridge, Mass.: Harvard University Press, 1931–58). A comprehensive 15 volume edition of Peirce's work is in preparation: see Bibliography, p. 161. James K. Feibleman's *An Introduction to Peirce's Philosophy* (London: Allen & Unwin, 1960) offers an extremely helpful commentary upon and systematization of Peirce's work. See particularly pp. 81–95 and 197 ff.

acts simply and singly (as indicated by the prefix *sin*) as a sign; and the *legisign*, a law that acts as a sign (i.e., not in the form of a single object but as the abstract working of a set of rules or principles: grammar operates as a recurring *legisign* in language).

(b) 'triadic relations of performance' involving actual entities in the real world, based on the kind of *ground*. These are the *icon*, something which functions as a sign by means of features of itself which resemble its object; the *index*, something which functions as a sign by virtue of some sort of factual or causal connection with its object; and the *symbol*, something which functions as a sign because of some 'rule' of conventional or habitual association between itself and its object.

(c) 'triadic relations of thought' based on the kind of *object*. These are the *rheme* (or *seme*), a sign which indicates the understood possibility of an object to the interpretant, should he have occasion to activate or invoke it; the *dicent* (or *dicisign* or *pheme*) which *conveys* information about its object, as opposed to a sign from which information may be derived; and the *argument*, a sign whose object is ultimately not a single thing but a *law*.

Peirce goes on to propose various possible combinations of the nine types of sign described above which would yield ten *classes* of sign: e.g., a dicent-symbol-legisign (a proposition); a rhematic-indexical-sinsign (a spontaneous cry); a dicent-indexical-sinsign (a weathercock) and so on. Combinations between the ten fundamental classes of signs ultimately yield sixty-six fuller classes of signs and various groups of these achieve fundamental importance in Peirce's analysis and systematization of logic.[1]

The complexity of Peirce's system clearly arises from the fact that, given his point of departure, anything which can be isolated, then connected with something else and 'interpreted', can function as a sign. This means that one of the most important areas in which his notion of signs will usefully operate will be that of epistemology: the analysis of the process of 'knowing' itself; of how knowledge is possible. Both for simplicity's sake, and because of its centrality to our

---

[1] For an extensive critique of Peirce's categories, see Umberto Eco, *op. cit.*, pp. 178 ff.

experience of the real world, most interpreters of Peirce have so far tended to limit their attention to the application of his theories in this area. According to Peirce, the framework for the existence of know-ledge derives from the assertion of propositions through the second 'triad' of signs: *icon, index* and *symbol*. Their importance thus requires us to take a closer look at them.

In the *icon*, the relationship between sign and object, or signifier and signified, manifests, to use Peirce's phrase, a 'community in some qual-ity': a similarity or 'fitness' of resemblance proposed by the sign, to be acknowledged by its receiver. Thus a diagram or a painting has an *iconic* relationship to its subject in so far as it resembles it: it is the signifier to its subject's signified in the *iconic* mode.

In the *index*, the relationship is concrete, actual and usually of a sequential, causal kind. The pointing finger is a signifier whose rela-tionship to its signified is *indexical* in mode. A knock on the door is an *index* of someone's presence, and the sound of a car's horn is a sign of the car's presence in the same mode. Smoke is an *index* of fire. A weathercock is an *index* of the direction of the wind.

In the *symbol* the relationship between signifier and signified is arbi-trary; it requires the active presence of the interpretant to make the signifying connection. And of course, following Saussure, we can say that the major systematic manifestation of signs in this mode occurs in language. Where my pointing finger, or my observation of a leaf could be said to be the *index* of a tree; where my painting or diagram of a tree constitutes an *icon* of the tree, my utterance of the word 'tree' (or *arbre*, or *baum*, or *arbor*) is a *symbol* of the tree because there is no inherent, necessary 'tree-like' quality in that signifier: its relationship to an actual tree remains fundamentally arbitrary (or 'imputed', to use Peirce's term) sustained only by the structure of the language in which it occurs, and which is understood by its interpretant, and not by reference to any area of experience beyond that.

It is important to note here that the 'triad' involves, not mutually exclusive *kinds* of sign, but three modes of a relationship between sign and object or signifier and signified which co-exist in the form of a hierarchy in which one of them will inevitably have dominance over the other two. As Jakobson observes, we can have symbolic icons, iconic symbols, etc., and the nature of a sign's ultimately dominant mode will depend finally on its *context* (a car's horn used, in a film, to indicate relief, safety, rather than danger, disaster, etc.). Thus a traffic signal may, in terms of epistemology, be said to combine *index* (pointing to a situation and calling for immediate, causally related action) and *symbol* (red, in our society, signals 'danger', 'stop'; green signals the opposite, and these arbitrarily related colours are binarily opposed by the traffic signalling system, as *symbols*).

Peirce's analysis tells us a good deal about the kinds of signs that exist, about the way signs work, and what sort of procedures govern the use we make of them. The immense importance of his theories and the complexity and range of his writings on the subject mean that the significance of his contribution to semiotic theory must be widely recognized. Presumably the recent and rapidly increasing surge of interest in the subject will ultimately acknowledge his true status.

Meanwhile, many other voices are heard,[1] and in the absence of a universally accepted theory of semiotics, we might now obtain some further helpful insights by turning back from America to Europe, and from one of Semiotics's 'founding fathers' to the other: to the model of linguistic communication suggested by Saussure.

One of Saussure's most powerful interpreters in the matter of semiotics has been Roland Barthes. In his essay 'Myth Today'[2] he puts the case that any semiotic analysis must postulate a relationship between the two terms *signifier* and *signified* which is not one of 'equality' but of 'equivalence'. What we *grasp* in the relationship is not the sequential ordering whereby one term *leads to* the other, but the correlation which *unites* them. In respect of language this (as I have termed it above) 'structural relationship' between sound-image (signifier) and concept (signified) constitutes what Saussure calls the *linguistic sign*. In respect of non-linguistic systems, says Barthes, this 'associative total' of signifier and signified constitutes simply the *sign*.

His example is a bunch of roses. It can be used to *signify* passion.

---

[1] A good idea of the range of recent work can be obtained from the two issues of the *Times Literary Supplement* devoted to the subject under the heading 'The Tell-Tale Sign: A Survey of Semiotics', 5th and 12th October, 1973. Umberto Eco's recent *A Theory of Semiotics*, gives a good, if rather abstract, account of the current 'state of play' and Pierre Guiraud's *Semiology*, though less up to date, tackles the central issues rewardingly.

[2] This forms the last section of *Mythologies*, pp. 109–59.

When it does so, the bunch of roses is the *signifier*, the passion the *signified*. The relation between the two (the 'associative total') produces the third term, the bunch of roses as a *sign*. And, *as a sign*, it is important to understand that the bunch of roses is quite a different thing from the bunch of roses as a signifier: that is, as a horticultural entity. As a *signifier*, the bunch of roses is *empty*, as a sign it is *full*. What has filled it (with signification) is a combination of my intent and the nature of society's conventional modes and channels which offer me a range of vehicles for the purpose. The range is extensive, but conventionalized and so finite, and it offers a complex system of ways of signifying:

> ... take a black pebble: I can make it signify in several ways, it is a mere signifier; but if I weigh it with a definite signified (a death sentence, for instance, in an anonymous vote), it will become a sign.
>
> (*Mythologies*, p. 113)

However, the process of signification does not end there. Barthes moves on to consider the ways in which 'myth' signifies in society (and by 'myth' he means, as we have seen above, not 'classical' mythology so much as the complex system of images and beliefs which a society constructs in order to sustain and authenticate its sense of its own being: i.e. the very fabric of its system of 'meaning').

In the case of myth, he argues, we find again the tripartite signifying operation described above: the signifier, the signified, and their product, the sign. However, myth is peculiar in that it invariably functions as a *second-order* semiotic system constructed on the basis of a semiotic chain which exists before it. That which had the status of a *sign* (i.e. the 'associative total' of signifier and signified) in the first system becomes a mere *signifier* in the second. Thus, where language provides a model for what we might call *primary* signification (as in the case of the bunch of roses), the model for *secondary* (or mythical) signification is more complex:

> Everything happens as if myth shifted the formal system of the first significations sideways. As this lateral shift is essential for the analysis of myth, I shall represent it in the following way, it being understood,

of course, that the spatialization of the pattern is here only a metaphor:

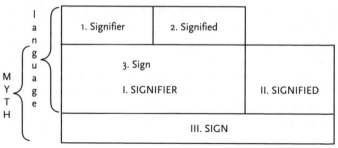

Mythologies, p. 115

In other words, myth operates by taking a previously established *sign* (which is 'full' of signification) and 'draining' it until it becomes an 'empty' *signifier*. One of Barthes's best-known examples is the following:

> I am at the barber's, and a copy of *Paris-Match* is offered to me. On the cover, a young Negro in a French uniform is saluting, with his eyes uplifted, probably fixed on a fold of the tricolour. All this is the *meaning* of the picture. But, whether naively or not, I see very well what it signifies to me: that France is a great Empire, that all her sons, without any colour discrimination, faithfully serve under her flag, and that there is no better answer to the detractors of an alleged colonialism than the zeal shown by this Negro in serving his so-called oppressors. I am therefore again faced with a greater semiological system: there is a signifier, itself already formed with a previous system (*a black soldier is giving the French salute*); there is a signified (it is here a purposeful mixture of Frenchness and militariness); finally, there is a presence of the signified through the signifier.
>
> (*Mythologies* p. 116)

Barthes goes on to propose that this third term in myth (which in language we would call the *sign*) should be called the *signification*, that the first term (signifier) should be called the *form* and that the second (the signified) should be called the *concept*. Thus, where in the first order of signification, that of language, the relation of *signifier* to *signified* generates the *sign*, in the *second* order of signification, that of myth, the relation of form (i.e. the first order's *sign*) to *concept* generates the *signification*.

With *signification* we have, of course, encountered an extremely powerful, because covert, producer of meaning at a level where an impression of 'god-given' or 'natural' reality prevails, largely because we are not normally able to perceive the processes by which it has been manufactured. Barthes's analysis of *semiosis*, in moving *via* Saussure on to this level, begins to take us 'behind the scenes' as it were of our own construction of the world.

The fruitfulness of this notion can be seen when Barthes applies it to the processes of signification which we traditionally term 'denotation' and 'connotation'. 'Denotation' we normally take to mean the use of language to mean what it says: 'connotation' means the use of language to mean something other than what is said. And, of course, 'connotation' is centrally characteristic of the 'literary' or 'aesthetic' use of language. In Barthes's view, connotation represents the same kind of 'gearing up' from denotation as myth does from ordinary signification. Thus, connotation takes place when the *sign* resulting from a previous signifier–signified relationship becomes the *signifier* of a further one.

> the first system is then the plane of *denotation* and the second system ... the plane of *connotation*. We shall therefore say that a *connoted system is a system whose plane of expression* (i.e. signifier) *is itself constituted by a signifying system*: the common cases of connotation will of course consist of complex systems of which language forms the first system (this is, for instance, the case with literature).[1]

In short, the *signifiers* of connotation are made up of the *signs* (signifiers related to signifieds) of the denoted system, and this makes connotation, and so literature at large, one of the numbers of 'second-order signifying systems' which we characteristically superimpose upon the 'first-order' system of language.

There is also a reverse situation in which the *sign* of a prior

---

[1] *Elements of Semiology*, pp. 89–90. The first parenthesis is my insertion.

signifier–signified relationship becomes the *signified* of a further one. In this case, the 'second-order' system becomes a *metalanguage*. This is the situation of semiotics itself. It acts as a *metalanguage* in respect of the *semiosis* which it studies.

Human beings emerge from any account of semiotic structures as inveterate and promiscuous producers of signs. As the work of Lévi-Strauss and others indicates, any aspect of human activity carries the potential for serving as, or becoming a sign; we only have to 'activate' it in accordance with something like the above processes. As Umberto Eco says, a sign is anything that can be taken as 'significantly substituting for something else'.[1] Accordingly, nothing in the human world can be *merely* utilitarian: even the most ordinary buildings organize space in various ways, and in so doing they signify, issue some kind of message about the society's priorities, its presuppositions concerning human nature, politics, economics, over and above their overt concern with the provision of shelter, entertainment, medical care, or whatever. All five senses, smell, touch, taste, hearing, sight, can function in the process of *semiosis*: that is, as sign-producers or sign-receivers. The uses of perfume, of the texture of a fabric in clothing, the ways in which the tastes produced by cooking signal status, location, 'identity', 'foreignness' are manifold. Moreover, each of these senses responds in concert with the others to sign-systems designed to exploit them in differing hierarchies. Conceivably there is a *langue* of cooking, of which each meal is a *parole*, and in connection with which *taste* is the sense most exploited, although *sight* and *smell* also have their role. Equally, there is no doubt a *langue* of perfume and, as Barthes has demonstrated at length (with complications, in his *Système de la Mode*) of 'fashion' and of writing about fashion at large.[2] Nevertheless, as Jakobson says, it is evident that 'the most socialized, abundant and pertinent sign systems in human society are based on sight and hearing' (*op. cit.*, p. 701).

Auditory signs are essentially different in character from visual signs. The first use time, not space, as a major structuring agent. The second use space rather than time. Auditory, 'temporal' signs tend to be sym-

[1] *Op. cit.*, p. 7.

[2] See Barthes's account of the 'signifying systems' of garments, food, cars and furniture, *Elements of Semiology*, pp. 25–30.

bolic in character: visual, 'spatial' signs tend to be iconic in character. The former signs, fully elaborated, yield in terms of art the major forms of spoken language and music. The latter, visual and spatial signs, yield the art-forms of painting, sculpture, architecture, etc. And of course, beyond these broad generalizations, there are forms of art which combine both: drama, opera, film, television etc.

The signs may be produced either *organically*, by the body, or *instrumentally*, by means of a technological extension of the body. Language is the most 'pure' organic semiotic system. Every aspect of it signifies, and it is produced solely by means of the body. When the 'extension' of the body, which we call a *medium*, causes one organic factor to become dominant over the others (the telephone has this effect on the voice: silent film had the same effect on bodily gesture) then it will inevitably affect the nature of the discourse. That is, the medium will begin to affect the message. When this takes extreme form, we find ourselves confronted, not with a medium which simply transmits a pre-packaged message, but with an *autonomous* semiotic system, with a 'life' – that is, with messages – of its own.

One of the most important examples of this process is the writing system of a language. Although we are, through long experience, habituated to our own writing system, there can be no doubt that it does not simply *record* our language. As Jakobson puts it

> Written language is prone to develop its peculiar structural properties so that the history of two chief linguistic varieties, speech and letters, is rich in dialectical tensions and alternations of mutual repulsions and attractions.
>
> (*op. cit.*, p. 706)

And so, when we take up the question of what semiotics can contribute to the study of literature, the 'peculiar structural properties' of writing clearly become crucial, as they form, semiotically, a large part of what any piece of writing communicates. Writing, after all, combines two kinds of sign. Language, which is normally *auditory* in mode, is made *visual* when it is written down or given printed form. To the auditory sign's commitment to *time* as its structuring agent is therefore added (and in one sense, the process is also one of reduction) the visual sign's commitment to *space*. Thus writing imposes on language a linearity and a sequentiality and a physical existence in space which speech does not have. Further, as we noticed above, auditory 'temporal' signs tend to be (in Peirce's terms) *symbolic* in character, where visual 'spatial' signs tend to be *iconic* in character. It follows that, in writing, both kinds of sign will always be present and capable of signification.

Thus, the two distinctive *genres* of language in its written form, poetry and prose, emit *iconic* messages about their nature through the visual means of typography over and above (or under and beneath) the *symbolic* messages of their content. A poem is 'set out' in a different form from that of a passage of prose: a novel 'looks like' a novel, not like a text-book. The writer can choose to increase the intensity of this *iconic* message, or to decrease it, in relation to the *symbolic* message emitted by the 'content' of the writing, depending upon the nature of the total message he intends.

The writer of, say, a detective novel, is normally concerned primarily with content, and would find any iconic message beyond that of 'this is a detective novel' to be merely an interference. On the other hand, a novelist like Joyce might wish to raise the iconic level of the total message so as to generate tension, irony, social comment, etc. So, in this passage from *Ulysses*, the iconic message 'this is a novel' suddenly changes:

> Oyster eyes. Never mind. Be sorry after perhaps when it dawns on him. Get the pull over him that way.
>
> Thank you. How grand we are this morning.
>
> ### IN THE HEART OF THE HIBERNIAN METROPOLIS
>
> BEFORE NELSON'S PILLAR TRAMS SLOWED, SHUNTED, CHANGED trolley, started for Blackrock, Kingstown and Dalkey, Clonskea, Rathgar and Terenure . . .
>
> ### THE WEARER OF THE CROWN
>
> Under the porch of the general post office shoeblacks called and polished . . .
>
> (*Ulysses*, pp. 107–8)

– and turns into 'this is a newspaper'.

Similarly, the following passage from Christine Brooke-Rose's novel THRU employs a high degree of iconic communication:

unless the mirror is moved to the

                                   sudden isolation

of seeing nothing whatever in the

                          rear

                  of

            the

        mind

    and

  no

narrator at all though this is only a manner of speaking since the text has somehow come into existence but with varying degrees of presence either bent or gazing into diasynchronic space or

at the chain of phonic signifiers
like Ali Nourennin the beardless
Marx who takes no notes and stares
with riveting eyes that break the
chain asunder with a listening look

But it needs adjusting. (p. 32)

In the following poems, both E. E. Cummings and William Carlos Williams rely on visual, iconic signs as important ingredients of the total message:

'next to of course god america i
love you land of the pilgrims' and so forth oh
say can you see by the dawn's early my
country 'tis of centuries come and go
and are no more what of it we should worry
in every language even deafanddumb
thy sons acclaim your glorious name by gorry
by jingo by gee by gosh by gum

> why talk of beauty what could be more beaut-iful
> than these heroic happy dead
> who rushed like lions to the roaring slaughter
> they did not stop to think they died instead
> then shall the voice of liberty be mute?'
>
> He spoke. And drank rapidly a glass of water
>
> e. e. cummings

> *This Is Just To Say*
> I have eaten
> the plums
> that were in
> the icebox
>
> and which
> you were probably
> saving
> for breakfast
>
> Forgive me
> they were delicious
> so sweet
> and so cold
>
> William Carlos Williams

Cummings's poem uses visual means to transmit the message 'this passage of writing is without form' (his habitual rendering of his own name, 'e. e. cummings' similarly represents a visual attempt at efface-ment of an intrusive ego). Meanwhile, on an auditory level, the 'poetic' form of the poem is of course the highly structured arrangement of rhymes and rhythms traditionally recognized as a sonnet. The message 'this is a sonnet' emitted in the *symbolic* mode is thus effectively seen to be overwhelmed by the message concerning formlessness (i.e. 'this is not a sonnet') emitted in the *iconic* mode just as – and this, presumably, is the 'total' message of the poem – inherited, traditional social forms are overwhelmed and muffled by the mouthings of the politician. The ultimate degradation brought about by war, it seems, lies in the disintegration of language's formal powers: the body of the poem's content is made up of the wreckage of patriotic songs and slogans.

In William Carlos Williams's poem, we see the process almost in reverse. Here the imposition of a new and disturbing status on what would otherwise remain a banal domestic piece of writing is brought about by the visual *iconic* message which says 'this passage of writing constitutes a poem': that is, 'these words have a significance beyond their overt meaning.' Meanwhile, the *symbolic* signs emitted lack any of the indications of 'poemness' that our culture leads us to look for and expect. By these means, the poem is able to make us think about what those expectations really are and whether or not we really endorse them. It even makes us think about the nature of the social conventions which invest 'poems' with 'significance', but deny it to other forms of utterance. In thus using *iconic* means to subvert our expectations, both poems prove fundamentally disturbing.[1]

This is not of course to say that, in referring more or less directly to themselves, such poems are in any way unusual. The case has more than once been made that all literary works of art are auto-referential to a certain degree. And it seems to follow that, given the dominance of the language-model, what is true of the 'aesthetic function' of language will also be true of the 'aesthetic function' of sign-systems at large. As Jakobson puts it,

> . . . introversive semiosis, a message which signifies itself, is indissolubly linked with the aesthetic function of sign-systems'.
>
> *(op. cit.,* p. 704)

In other words, if literature consists at least in part of signs that do not signify in the 'normal' way because they signify themselves, then

[1] Cf. Culler's interesting discussion of Williams's poem (op. cit., pp. 175–6) to which the above account is really a response. It will be clear that although I agree that 'when it is set down on the page as a poem the convention of significance comes into play', I do not accept Culler's conclusion that 'we must therefore supply a new function to justify the poem'. The poem's 'justification' seems to me to reside in its implicit questioning of the 'convention of significance'. It is about its own status and the social processes that determine our response to its language.

the 'aesthetic function' of all other sign-systems can perhaps be said systematically to involve breaking the 'rules' of signification in the same way. Moreover, the 'rules' not only require a signifier, or *signans* to refer beyond itself to a signified or *signatum*, they require it to do so unambiguously. Yet, in the aesthetic use of language, signifiers manifest, as we have seen, a high degree of 'plurality': that is, of ambiguity. And, as Umberto Eco comments, 'Semiotically speaking, ambiguity must be defined as a mode of violating the rules of the code.'[1]

It seems to follow that a semiotic analysis of all 'aesthetic functions' must in one sense see in them a paradoxical institutionalization of rule-breaking (a concept not very far distant, it will be remembered, from the view expressed by Jakobson that poetry represents 'organized violence committed on ordinary speech'). Art seen thus appears as a way of connecting 'messages' together, in order to produce 'texts' in which the 'rule-breaking' roles of ambiguity and self-reference are fostered and 'organized' so that, as Umberto Eco sees it,

(a) many messages on different levels are ambiguously organized
(b) the ambiguities follow a precise design
(c) both the normal and ambiguous devices in any one message exert a contextual pressure on the normal and ambiguous devices in all the others
(d) the way in which the 'rules' of one system are violated by one message is the same as that in which the rules of other systems are violated by their messages.[2]

The effect is to generate an 'aesthetic idiolect', a 'special language' peculiar to the work of art, which induces in its audience a sense of 'cosmicity' – that is, of endlessly moving beyond each established level of meaning the moment it is established – of continuously transforming 'its denotations into new connotations'. In fact, the process has many similarities to the one described by Barthes in his account of myth, where what has been established as a *sign* on one level

---

[1] Umberto Eco, *op. cit.*, p. 262.
[2] *Op. cit.*, p. 271.

of signification can be 'drained' so that it can then become a *signifier* on *another* level, and it obviously confirms Barthes's account of connotation as a 'second order' system of signification based upon denotation. Eco seems to be suggesting that the aesthetic message operates as a continuing 'multi-order' system of signification which moves from level to level, its denotations becoming connotations in a kind of infinite progression. As a result, we never arrive at a 'final' decoding or 'reading' of the aesthetic message, because each ambiguity generates further cognate 'rule-breaking' at other levels, and invites us continuously to dismantle and reassemble what the work of art seems at any point to be 'saying':

> common artistic experience also teaches us that art not only elicits feelings but also *produces further knowledge*. The moment that the game of intertwined interpretations gets under way, the text compels one to reconsider the usual codes and their possibilities.
>
> (p. 274)

The process has obvious affinities with the one used by Barthes in S/Z. As a result of it, the reader becomes more and more aware of the new 'semiotic possibilities' available within the codes. He is forced in consequence to 'rethink' their whole arrangement and, ultimately, that of the 'reality' which they encode for him. Thus, to use Barthes's terms, in his new-found capacity as *écrivain*, the reader not only begins to 'see the world' differently, he learns how to create a new world: 'By increasing one's knowledge of codes, the aesthetic message changes one's view of their history and thereby *trains* semiosis' (p. 274). The aesthetic message, then, exhibits the same double function as any language: it is both affective (or emotive) and cognitive in mode.[1] We are back, in a sense, with Vico and with Lévi-Strauss. Like myth, art represents, not the mere

---

[1] See Pierre Guiraud's argument that, in terms of semiotics, the modes of any culture's range of experience are deployed in terms of two 'poles', the cognitive mode and the affective mode. Their relationship is inversely proportional (the more an experience inclines to one the less it will incline to the other) and never mutually exclusive. They manifest themselves in signifying systems principally by means of two similarly related expressive functions: the referential (cognitive) function and the emotive (affective) function. *Semiology*, pp. 9–18.

'embroidery' of reality, but a way of knowing it, of coping with it, and of changing it.

This is not to deny that major modes of art will appear to involve an apparently straightforward and stable commitment to an unchanging world 'beyond' themselves. A book of a certain kind will always appear as a window through which such a world is clearly visible. In it, the signifiers appear to point directly and confidently to the signifieds. But a central tenet of structuralism and semiotics is, as we have seen, that even in cases where the aim of the work is utter realism (the detective novel, Balzac's *Sarrasine*), this 'transparency' of writing, this 'innocence' of literature, remains an illusion. Writing in a work of fiction (an 'epistolary' novel called *Zoo: or letters not about love*, 1923) the Russian formalist critic Viktor Shklovsky typically forces the work to reveal its own lack of innocence or transparency by making its central character (a man writing letters to his loved one) continually refer to the necessary self-reflexive character of all art:

> There are two attitudes toward art.
>
> One is to view the work of art as a window on the world.
>
> Through words and images, these artists want to express what lies beyond words and images. Artists of this type deserve to be called translators.
>
> The other type of attitude is to view art as a world of independently existing things.
>
> Words, and the relationships between words, thoughts and the irony of thoughts, their divergence – these are the content of art. Art, if it can be compared to a window at all, is only a sketched window.
>
> (*Zoo: or letters not about love*, trans. Richard Sheldon, p. 8o)

The reference to the 'sketched window' of art has of course a telling semiotic effect when it occurs in the middle of that most 'window-like' of art-forms, the novel made out of letters: in this case some of them apparently *actual* letters exchanged between Shklovsky and a specific woman, and one of them (in a perfect example of 'rule-breaking' ambiguity) even 'crossed out' – although it remains perfectly legible – with the reader advised to 'skip' it. No writing, such a work clearly states, can be transparent: *all* writing (even when 'obliterated') signifies. The moment it does so, it becomes a formative, mediating agency. In the process, actual letters are turned into 'literature', truth becomes fiction, 'real life' becomes part of a novel. And so, despairingly, the central character can complain

> How I want simply to describe objects as if literature had never existed; that way one could write literarily.

(p. 84)

But of course, that kind of pristine 'literariness' is no longer available. We can never now use words as if literature had never existed.

The claims some literature makes to originality, to realism, to physical accuracy of description have ultimately to be seen in this depleting light. To the semiotician, most works of literature, in emitting messages that refer to themselves, also make constant reference to other works of literature. As Julia Kristeva has pointed out, no 'text' can ever be completely 'free' of other texts. It will be involved in what she has termed the *intertextuality* of all writing.

This leads to one of the most important insights into the nature of literature that semiotics affords. For books finally appear to portray or reflect, not the real physical world, but a world reduced to other dimensions; to the shape and structures of the activity of writing: the world as a text. Yet, surprisingly, literature remains, at least in the West, a centrally *privileged* form of signification. Our education system (and, some would add, the political system that authenticates it, and that is reinforced by it) continues to promote a 'literary' version of the world as 'real', gives it a dominant, formative status, and requires all other possible versions of the world to accommodate themselves to its shape. As a result, we tend to 'literarize' all our experience, reduce it to a kind of 'book': a process that, it has been argued, has been continuous with us since the renaissance and the concomitant development of the book-industry.[1] Yet, if everything is capable of signification, why *should* the literary mode be dominant? What is the nature of its domination? And what are

---

[1] See Marshall McLuhan, *The Gutenberg Galaxy* (London: Routledge, 1962), *passim*.

the effects on us of what Jakobson called the written sign's 'peculiar structural properties'?

One of the most interesting arguments concerning this aspect of the semiotics of writing has been offered by Jacques Derrida, who proposes a 'science' of the written sign, called *grammatology*. His three books, *De La Grammatologie, L'Ecriture et la Différence* and *La Voix et le phénomène* (all published in 1967) in fact represent a sustained argument for a reassessment of the nature and status of writing: a plea for writing to be considered, not as, traditionally, the external 'dress' of speech, a reduced 'coded' version of the voice whose 'pure' presence in its oral-aural manifestation is usually given primacy (as, for instance, Plato recommends in the *Phaedrus*) but as an entity in itself.

Our traditional commitment to the voice as the primary communicative instrument also commits us, in Derrida's view, to a falsifying 'metaphysics of presence', based on an illusion that we are able, ultimately, to 'come face to face once and for all with objects'.[1] That is, that some final, objective, unmediated 'real world' exists, about which we can have concrete knowledge. Derrida sees this belief in 'presence' as the major factor limiting our apprehension of the world: a distorting insistence that, in spite of our always fragmentary experience, somewhere there must exist a redeeming and justifying *wholeness*, which we can objectify in ourselves as the notion of Man, and beyond ourselves as the notion of Reality. This yearning underwrites and guarantees the belief that *necessary* connections exist between signifier and signified, and that these are ultimately locked in a 'meaningful', wholly unbreakable, real-world-generating union.[2]

However, Derrida argues, this 'humanist' view of the world, its centre 'Man', and European Man at that, has, in our century, finally reached its conclusion. And the break-up of this world in fact results in the break-up of European Man's inherited system of signifier-signified links. For if there exists no transcendental, ultimate, and so dominating

---

[1] Jameson, *The Prison-House of Language*, p. 173. Jameson's discussion of Derrida (pp. 173–86) is particularly valuable, as is Culler's, *op. cit.*, pp. 131–3, 243–5, 247–9. See also Jean-Marie Benoist, 'The End of Structuralism', *Twentieth Century Studies*, No. 3, May 1970, pp. 31–53. Derrida's own short essay 'La Différance' in *Tel Quel: Théorie d'Ensemble* (Paris: Seuil, 1968), pp. 41–66, contains some of his central ideas in summary form.

[2] See *L'Ecriture et la Différence*, pp. 41–4 and 409–11.

signified – i.e. 'human nature' – then the whole sphere of signification must be vastly extended. The world ceases to be limited to, and determined by, an inherited pattern of meanings, a traditional word/ meaning 'grid'. It ceases, that is, to be *phonocentric*. This break-up, and the consequent extension of 'meaning's' potential, can be fostered and encouraged through the analysis of *writing*.

Derrida's work can therefore be linked with that of Barthes as indicative of the kind of stress semiotics places on writing's distinctive and newly extended character. Once a 'science of signs' has demonstrated that the sign-system of writing does not act simply as a transparent window on to an established 'reality', it can be identified as a sign-system in its own right, with its own properties and its own distinct character.

This has various effects. Primarily, it raises our level of 'awareness' about the nature of the written or printed word. We begin, for instance, to recognize the extent to which all written words deal in and involve overt or suppressed images of the process of writing (a good example is William Carlos Williams's poem *This Is Just To Say* quoted above, but the most cursory glance at some of the traditional 'conventions' of the novel will make the same point: the 'epistolary' mode, the use of the 'intrusive' or 'omniscient' author, the sort of devices presented and mocked in Sterne's *Tristram Shandy* all confirm it). We also begin to recognize the extent to which the status of the written word has hitherto derived from European culture's sense of itself as truly definitive of Man's role in the world. The commitment of European education systems, by and large, to literacy as a primary skill – the only skill for a good deal of their history that has been fostered and rewarded – reveals a presupposition of immense proportions. But most important, the conclusion emerges that writing need no longer be considered as a *substitute* for something else that lies beyond it: a signifier in search of a signified, strung between the two poles of 'affective' and 'cognitive', 'emotive' and 'referential', fiction and fact, a secondary element for ever acting as the 'dress' of a primary 'presence'.

In place of this now eroded notion of the written word, Derrida introduces a concept deriving from an identity of what (in French) he terms *différence* and *différance*.

Différence (in English *differentiation*) represents the principle by which language works: that is, the process we have referred to as 'binary opposition', or the perception of phonemic differences between sounds. As Saussure puts it, 'in language there are only differences'. To differ or differentiate, Derrida argues, is also to defer (the English sense of the French différance is defer-ment): to postpone; to hold back; to propose a distinction between entities such as will enable one to refer to the other, or to be distinguished from it. That is, it represents involvement in a structuring process.

Derrida argues that the 'deferring' process in which writing appears to be involved – the written word acting as surrogate for the spoken word – in fact applies to the spoken word itself. That is, language's grounding in différence (or distinctions) also implies a commitment to différence (or deferring). Thus, speech cannot stand as the reality to writing's shadow, for speech already itself appears to be a shadow of some prior act of signification, of which it manifests the 'trace', and so on, in an infinite regression. In fact nothing has the 'purity' of absolute presence. Speech is as 'impure', as 'trace'-ridden, as 'secondary' as any sign-system. Thus, when I say 'tree' I am as distant from the actual physical entity growing in the earth as I am when I write 'tree'.

Moreover, by analysing writing, I am able to analyse the process by which language works because, far from being speech's shadow, writing captures language's essence. By virtue of its existence at one remove from any outside 'reality' (although obviously it gestures in that reality's direction) writing offers a model of language's nature.

Finally, the character of writing also generates a permanent gap between any text and any unitary 'meaning'. If the text and its 'meaning' are not one and the same thing (and the 'deferring' nature of writing, as Derrida sees it, makes this impossible) then a text can have no ultimate, final meaning: in fact, it is in the nature of writing, and of language, not to be confined to specific structures of meaning.[1]

Of course, this opens the door, not only for the kind of analysis at which Barthes has proved adept, but also for politically minded analysts (e.g. those who write for the journal Tel Quel) to claim with Philippe Sollers that, in a society which has imposed and institutionalized the written form of language as an overall dominating feature of

[1] See L'Ecriture et la différence, p. 411 and De la Grammatologie, p. 74 ff.

its way of life, all writing is political writing: 'Writing is the continuation of politics by other means.'[1]

But its full significance lies in the fact that this view of writing and of language frees the sign from its subservience to that 'reality' (or presence) which it was supposed to serve. Seen thus, writing emerges as *sui generis*: its own 'thing', not the creature of some superior reality. Writing, in short, does not 'reproduce' a reality beyond itself, nor does it 'reduce' that reality. In its new freedom, it can be seen to *cause a new reality to come into being*.[2]

Grammatology, says Derrida, would be the science of the written sign conceived in this way: the way in which writing has always been conceived (he claims) in oriental societies. Its terms, its conditions, its presuppositions, are not those of a dominant oral version of language, but those of writing itself. It communicates, not as a surrogate for the voice, not orally, but visually and *legibly*, in the way that, as we have seen, Christine Brooke-Rose's novel THRU does. And writing of this kind (the work of authors such as Joyce, Becket, Mallarmé, Robbe-Grillet and, earlier, Sterne come to mind) demands a criticism genuinely suited to its nature.

Traditional critical responses will yield very little. What the semiotic account of *any* writing needs, and certainly what writing conceived in that light requires, is something, perhaps, like Barthes's S/Z. As Georges Poulet has described it, it requires a special sense of reading:

> The work lives its own life within me; in a certain sense, it thinks itself, and it even gives itself a meaning within me.[3]

– a sense which takes account of the fact that, in one way, the work reads *us* as much as we read it. And that situation obviously calls for a quite different kind of criticism, of the sort that Poulet terms a

---

[1] Philippe Sollers, 'Ecriture et Révolution' in *Tel Quel: Théorie d'Ensemble* (Paris: Seuil, 1968), p. 78.

[2] It might then, according to Philippe Sollers, make common cause with revolution, as a kind of ideal 'red text' (*récit rouge*). *Théorie d'Ensemble*, p. 79.

[3] Georges Poulet, 'Criticism and the experience of interiority' in Richard Macksey and Eugenio Donato, eds., *The Structuralist Controversy*, p. 62.

total critical act: that is to say, the exploration of that mysterious inter-relationship which, through the mediation of reading and of language, is established to our mutual satisfaction between the work read and myself.[1]

[1] Ibid., p. 67.

5

CONCLUSIONS: NEW 'NEW CRITICISM' FOR OLD 'NEW CRITICISM'?

POSSIBLY the major instance so far of the 'total critical act' called for by Poulet remains Barthes's S/Z. A final task of this book, therefore, is to try to situate that work, its implications and the criticism that will surely follow it, in a context which will highlight the particular contributions structuralism and semiotics have made and will continue to make to the nature of our concept of and response to literature. One obvious feature shared by these new ways of thinking about writing and reading is a sense of an urgent, if somewhat unfocused, need for radical change.

'NEW CRITICISM'

Part of the difficulty of pinpointing the nature of the change needed arises, oddly enough, as a simple matter of nomenclature. The 'old' critical orthodoxy which requires replacement goes, paradoxically, by the name of 'New' Criticism.

New Criticism was itself conceived in opposition to an 'older' criticism which, in Britain and America in the late nineteenth and early twentieth centuries, had largely concerned itself with material extrane-ous to the work under discussion: with the biography and psychology of its author, or with the work's relationship to 'literary history'. The general principles of New Criticism can be simply formulated. The work of art, it proposed, and in particular the work of literary art, should be regarded as autonomous, and so should not be judged by reference to criteria or considerations beyond itself. It warrants noth-ing less than careful examination in and on its own terms. A poem consists, less of a series of referential and verifiable statements about the 'real' world beyond it, than of the presentation and sophisticated organization of a set of complex experiences in a verbal form. The critic's quarry is that complexity. It yields itself to close analytic read-ing without overt reference to any acknowledged 'method' or 'system' and without drawing on any corpus of information, biographical, social, psychological or historical, *outside* the work. 'There is no method' said T. S. Eliot (a poet and critic much favoured by New Criticism), 'except to be very intelligent.' As a result, an apparently 'free-floating' uncommitted critical intelligence directly confronts the unmediated 'word on the page': its reading proves sensitive to those devices concerned with the expansion or disintegration of referential meaning (e.g. ambiguity, paradox, irony, punning, 'wit') and is accordingly disposed to applaud stylistic qualities which foster them (e.g. 'intellectual toughness', 'tension'). It never goes 'beyond' the work to validate its arguments.

Obviously (though unknowingly) related to Russian Formalism, criticism of this kind flourished and grew in Britain and America in the 1930s and 1940s, to the extent that, by the mid 1950s, it had become, in the English speaking world at any rate, an established orthodoxy. 'New' Criticism was criticism itself. Its fundamental ideo-logical underpinning lay in notions of the values of 'tradition', and of 'rooted' organic community life in which complex levels of social interaction wove a deeply satisfying sense of an inherited reality of fixed, permanent dimensions. The cultural richness available in that life (and embodied above all in its literature) was felt properly to militate against any 'reduced' single vision or (it sometimes seemed) purpose. And so, from I. A. Richards's notion of a psychological 'complexity' at work in poem and experience, whereby a fruitful tension between opposing impulses organizes and refines them, and thus enables the reader to abstain from reductive action in either direction, to Cleanth Brooks's and William Empson's notion of a multiplicity of meaning available in words and their poetic usage, whereby fruitful ambiguity maintains a 'balance', enabling the reader to avoid a reductive opting for single meaning, this ideological commitment to equipoise found itself transformed into a range of unquestioned critical presuppositions. The poem seen thus becomes self-maintaining; a 'closed' area, a verbal icon. And the general drift of criticism in this form has been towards a sense of complexity on the one hand and of self-sustaining detachment on the other: away from 'unbalanced' commitment and simplifying involvement. Accordingly, its psychological mode is one of subjectivity. In fact, as Barthes points out, literature's current social function in this respect has become central: 'literature is that ensemble of objects and rules, techniques and works, whose function in the general economy of our society is precisely to institutionalize subjectivity' (Sur Racine, pp. 171–2). Its political and social modes are, appropriately, those of liberal humanism.

Most of the arguments that can be directed against New Criticism have already been mentioned in connection with the work of Roland Barthes. Barthes's total lack of reverence for the 'text' represents, of course, a frontal assault on New Criticism's first principle, which is that discussion should severely limit itself to an objective analysis of the 'words on the page'. We can perhaps summarize his arguments in the form of four principles:

(1) the principle that the 'innocent' reader (that unlikely belle sauvage, sans prejudice, ideology, commitment or stock response, whose ghostly rebuking presence stalks the pages of Practical Criticism) cannot and does not exist: it is not possible simply to confront the 'words on the page'. A whole world of mediating presuppositions of an economic, social, aesthetic and political order intervenes between us and them and shapes our response: to deny this is simply self-deceiving. (2) There exists consequently no 'objective' text and no pre-ordained 'content' stored within it. As Jakobson has pointed out, the 'poetic' function of language 'by promoting the palpability of signs, deepens the fundamental dichotomy of signs and

objects'.[1] Thus, no signifier is ineluctably tied to its signified. Following Jakobson, Barthes insists on the work of literature's commitment to self-reference. It is not a medium for a pre-packaged 'message': message and medium are one. Of course, New Criticism acknowledges this situation to a considerable degree, but its insistence on the sanctity of the text and the informality of the critical process proves finally at odds with it. In rejecting the notion of literature as an aspect of biography, psychology, or 'literary history', New Criticism admittedly turned literature into something autonomous, but it was also something strangely abstract, divorced from the concrete 'real life' of its author and audience. As Serge Doubrovsky puts it, where 'literary history' means authors without works, 'New Criticism' has tended to mean works without authors.[2] (3) The concomitant principle reinforced by the work of Derrida, that writing and reading are not the 'natural' processes that liberal humanism (characteristically anaesthetized to the implications of much of its own technology) presupposes – and (4) the final principle, matching the first, that all critical positions and judgements in fact mask a complex political and economic ideology: there is no 'neutral' or 'innocent' critical position.

This latter point derives ultimately from Marxist theory, which would see New Criticism as one of the ideological outgrowths of capitalism; dependent upon the 'real foundations' of its economic ordering of the world, and covertly reflecting and reinforcing these, while overtly it appears to address itself to quite other matters. Thus, New Criticism's admiration of complexity, balance, poise and tension could be said to sustain the characteristic bourgeois concern for a 'fixed' and established, unchanging reality, because it disparages forceful, consistent and direct action. Although opposed to 'referential' critical acts, which go 'beyond' the poem's context, New Criticism proves highly selective in respect of what it considers that 'context' to be. Its presuppositions, Barthes argues, about the nature of man's moral, psychological and social being are all too evident in its scarcely concealed assumptions involving matters such as 'taste' and 'sensitivity' and its

---

[1] Jakobson, 'Closing statement', op. cit., p. 356. See above, p. 86.
[2] Serge Doubrovsky, The New Criticism in France, p. 114.

habit of speaking of these as if they were objective and unchanging human qualities, unaffected by historical and economic pressures. This forms part of what Barthes dismisses as 'dishonest' criticism, based on the supposition that the work criticized exists in some objective concrete way *before* the critical act; that, however complex or ambiguous it may be, it can ultimately be reduced to a univocal 'content' beyond which it is improper to go. Thus, New Criticism's high regard for 'ambiguity', its admiration of polysemous structures, represent no real leaning towards 'total' criticism so much as a bourgeois mistrust of singlemindedness and commitment: the stances it prizes most − sophistication, wit, poise − are those of a decaying aristocracy characteristically revered by a sycophantic middle-class.

Whatever we may think of the sort of necessary connection between sub-structure and super-structure this implies, the process also perhaps works the other way. The attitudes implicit in New Criticism itself may, in turn, be said to have been influential on the 'real foundations'. How many, one wonders, of the civil servants, the teachers, the journalists who generate the climate of opinion that ultimately shapes the actions of politicians and generals, derive at least some elements in their total view of life from experiences whose essence is literary? Mass literacy, and an education system firmly based on it, has tended in twentieth century Europe and America to establish and reinforce an equation between literature and life that would have astonished any preceding age. When that equation comes, through the mediation of literary criticism, to acquire positive prescriptive force in respect of morality, politics, even economics, and when its presuppositions find themselves transmitted at large and unquestioned throughout an all-embracing system of education, then it seems reasonable to expect that 'crises' in one area will find themselves mirrored in another.

Eventually, the sense of crisis proves to be the agency which generates the need for change. When liberal humanism in America and Western Europe encountered the series of debilitating post-war crises of conscience that ran from Algeria to Suez to Vietnam, then the criticism which sustained that humanism, and which was sustained by it, was similarly shaken. In short, the students who rejected liberal politics in the nineteen-sixties as a mystified game, rejected liberal (so-called 'practical') criticism as part of the same package. It seemed no less of a game: literally ludicrous.

'NEW' NEW CRITICISM

What has a 'new' New Criticism to offer then, as a replacement for an old and discredited New Criticism? Certainly, Barthes and others are prepared to embrace the *total* implications of the work of art's self-referentiality without any limits imposed by a sense of an ultimate 'objective' or concrete reality beyond itself to which the work must be seen to refer. 'New' New Criticism would thus claim to respond to literature's essential nature in which signifiers are prised utterly free of signifieds, aiming, in its no-holds-barred encounter with the text, for a *coherence* and *validity* of response, not objectivity and truth. The most important feature of this process is that it offers a new role and status to the critic. It makes him a participant in the work he reads. The critic *creates* the finished work by his reading of it, and does not remain simply the inert *consumer* of a 'ready-made' product. Thus the critic need not humbly efface himself before the work and submit to its demands: on the contrary, he actively constructs its meaning: he *makes* the work exist; 'there is no Racine *en Soi* . . . Racine exists in the readings of Racine, and apart from the readings there is no Racine.'[1] None of these readings is *wrong*, they all add to the work. So, a work of literature ultimately consists of *everything* that has been said about it. As a result, no work ever 'dies': 'A work is eternal not because it imposes a single meaning on different men, but because it suggests different meanings to a single man, speaking the same symbolic language in all ages: the work proposes, man disposes.'[2] Barthes's *S/Z* remains the exhilarating monument to this 'total' rejection of the critic's passive role. To this one should add Barthes's concomitant insistence on a new emphasis on literature as it *really* is: a signifying system which characteristically and autonomously employs the specific activities of reading and writing, and which is not simply concerned to deliver a pre-ordained 'content' to the reader.

[1] Doubrovsky, *op. cit.*, p. 7.
[2] Roland Barthes, *Critique et vérité*, p. 51.

> ... we have not been able to recognise clearly the nature of the literary *object*, which is a written object. From the moment that one admits that the work is made with writing (and draws the consequences from that admission) then a *certain* science of literature becomes possible ... This cannot be a science of content ... but a science of the *conditions* of content, that is, a science of forms.[1]

In pursuit of that 'science of forms' and in place of a criticism obsessed with *content*, endlessly aiming to exhibit its own 'sensitivity', or to discover facts about the author's psychology, or the 'real world' beyond, or to assign unitary concrete and permanent 'meanings' to works of literature, Jonathan Culler has recently proposed.

> ... a poetics which strives to define the conditions of meaning. Granting new attention to the activity of reading, it would attempt to specify how we go about making sense of texts, what are the interpretive operations on which literature itself, as an institution, is based.[2]

The key concept is obviously that of 'poetics': a concern, not with *content*, but with the *process* by which content is formulated. It rests on an analogy made with one of the fundamental developments of modern linguistics: the notion that the central task of linguistic investigation is not, ultimately, to describe a corpus of data, but 'to account for facts about language by constructing a formal representation of what is involved in knowing a language' (p. 26). Applied to literature, this model suggests that 'a text can be a poem only because certain possibilities exist within the tradition: it is written in relation to other poems' (p. 30). In short, criticism needs a Saussure. For just as linguistics attempts to account for an abstract system (*langue*/competence) which generates the concrete event (*parole*/performance) so literary criticism should attempt to account for a 'poetics' of writing and

---

[1] *Op. cit.*, pp. 56–7. Both these passages from *Critique et vérité* are subjected to valuable scrutiny by Gabriel Josipovici in *The World and the Book*, pp. 264 and 270. I recommend his treatment of the subject at large, pp. 256–85.

[2] Jonathan Culler, *Structuralist Poetics*, p. viii.

reading, conceived as an abstract system of conventions, by whose means 'poems', 'novels' etc. are generated, and are perceived as such by members of the culture involved.

Raising his sights from the level established by previous structuralists who have been largely concerned with individual literary perform-ances and the development of discovery procedures appropriate to them, Culler aims to establish a concept of literary 'competence' cap-able of generating all the elements of the edifice that we collectively recognize as literature. He thus attempts to make explicit the under-lying 'set of conventions for reading literary texts' that would consti-tute such competence (p. 118). These, after all, are the conventions that permit us to 'make sense' of poetry, and the fact that it is possible – however generally – to formulate them; e.g. the 'rule of significance' (which requires the poem to be read as expressing a 'significant' atti-tude to some large problem), the 'rule of metaphorical coherence' (which insists that the two component aspects of the metaphor exhibit some consistent relationship) and the 'rule of thematic unity' (which we learn to look for, applaud, and so construct) enable the argument to focus rewardingly on the nature of writing as a social institution and of reading as a social activity.

Following Derrida, Culler's structuralist commitment reveals itself to best advantage in his insistence that writing cannot be treated on the model of speech. The written word (the stuff of literature) is independent of the 'presence' of a speaker, and as an object in its own right enjoys an autonomous 'productivity'. That is, it characteristically subjects the overt signifier-signified ligament to a covert and poten-tially dislocating strain, finally making it possible to 'free' the one from the other. If man merely *complies* with the structure of his language to an extent that justifies Heidegger's assertion 'language speaks, not man', the same principle forces a similar conclusion in respect of literature: writing writes, not authors. So, writing's autonomy in respect of the signifier-signified connection ultimately yields the fundamental paradox of literature:

> . . . its formal and fictional qualities bespeak a strangeness, a power, an organization, a permanence which is foreign to ordinary speech. Yet the urge to assimilate that power and permanence or to let that

> formal organization work upon us requires us to make literature into a
> communication, to reduce its strangeness . . .
>
> (p. 134)

The means whereby that 'reduction' takes place must then become a major element in the design of a 'poetics' appropriate to our culture.

As the age of Western European technological and cultural pre-eminence recedes, so the communicative, mediating modes promoted by that pre-eminence emerge as the partial, distorting agencies they are. Structuralism's distinctive contribution to literary criticism may well lie, as has been said, in its recognition of the nature and implications of those modes in the particular form of the acts of reading and writing, and of their function in the institutionalizing process that has generated our notion of literature.

It follows that if we can construct what Culler calls 'a poetics which stands to literature as linguistics stands to language'[1], we shall come closer to an understanding of the theory of the practice of reading and writing: that is, of one of the fundamental processes that finally defines us. And this, ultimately, is the goal to which structuralist criticism ought to be directed: 'to read the text as an exploration of writing, of the problems of articulating a world'.[2] How we articulate our world determines, as Vico discovered, how we arrive at what we call reality. There could be no more crucial objective for any discipline.

[1] *Op. cit.*, p. 257.
[2] *Ibid.*, p. 260.

AFTERWORD

'Congratulations'

'Thank you'

'Now: do you mind if I bring up something that's rather personal?'

'Not at all'

'I was wondering if you planned to do anything about . . . well, about your accent?'

'Er . . .?'

'Well, you are going to be teaching English after all'

It was 1955. I'd just huffed and puffed my way over the final hurdles leading to a slightly shady Bachelor's degree in the subject known as 'English language and literature'. The enquiry came from my tutor. Of course, I knew only too well what he meant. But at that age, I was bloody-minded enough to let what I thought of as 'the facts' speak for me. Accent? Mine couldn't have been a more English one. I'd just spoken and could not speak any language other than English. I was born, raised, and had gone to school right in the middle of England: in Birmingham, about twenty-five miles from Shakespeare's birthplace. Both my parents were English. I spoke the language like a native and my accent was unmistakable. It announced my Midlands origin with an ancient cadence. I *was* a native, for heaven's sake! A Brummie.

But that was really the problem. In those days, being a native speaker certainly didn't guarantee that you spoke the language properly. In fact, to speak it as I did was regarded by some as scarcely to speak English at all. The penalties incurred by intonations of the Brummie sort were appropriately severe. Peremptory exclusion from the realm of the 'educated' was the least of them. The attention of offenders might be brusquely drawn to the instruments of phonetic cleansing glinting menacingly in the corner of Nurse's room. Carbolic early-morning regimes of industrial-strength vowel-laundering could easily loom. To propose (as I once did) that the Bard himself – my fellow Midlander – might have sounded a bit like me, was to dice with retribution of a well-honed physical and spiritual sort. Reaching for his cane, my empurpled headmaster asked if I was a communist.

In the event, history rather than MI5 came to the rescue. Although, on a conscious level, I deliberately did nothing about it, my accent nevertheless underwent the standard phonetic attrition of the years: first erosion and then replacement by a mixture of the sibilants of South Wales, the aspirates of America, and the myriad syllabic adjustments fostered by appetite, vanity, and zealous resort to dance-hall, jazz-club and cinema. Finally, the whirligig of time emphatically brought in his revenges when, at the end of the first class I ever taught in a university in upstate New York, a student congratulated me on the way I spoke, terming it 'wonderful', and adding that I sounded just like David Niven.

Talk about the kiss of death. But I am now able, on reflection, to recognise in that exchange a livelier element that strikes me as rather more significant: an initial and formative encounter with one of the first principles of structuralism. At an early stage of this book, I sketch out the case that what we think of as reality lies 'not in things themselves, but in the relationships which we construct, and then perceive, between them' (p. 7). This, I argue, supports a way of looking at the world in which 'the nature of every element in any given situation has no significance by itself, and is in fact determined by its relationship to all the other elements involved in that situation . . .' As a result, 'the full significance of any entity or experience cannot be perceived unless and until it is integrated into the structure of which it forms a part' (p. 7). Above all, I conclude, this seems to be the case in respect of language.

In these terms, my convergence with the New World can be said to have had a manifestly structuralist tinge. It certainly involved language. It placed particular emphasis on the complex role played by speech in the operation of a specific culture or way of life. And one conclusion was inescapable. My accent undoubtedly signalled something, but its message was neither given nor unchanging. In fact, depending on its location, in Britain or in the United States, it could evidently transmit quite opposite 'meanings'. These seemed to derive, not from my vowel and consonant sounds in themselves, but entirely from the structure of the culture within which they were uttered and to which they were directed. Thus it seemed that, regardless of my headmaster's worries about Bolshevik insurgency, my accent conveyed, in itself, no essential message at all. Indeed, the very idea of its existence 'in itself' began to seem rather problematical. It suddenly appeared – in upstate New York of all places – that a tyranny which for generations had branded me and my fellow Brummies forcefully on the tongue might readily be overthrown. To some extent a prolonged celebration of that feeling of release still animates this book. And I'd be surprised if a similar sense of gleeful ungagging were not still just about discernible in the purpose and the title of the series in which it first appeared.

To generalise: if, before the nineteen-sixties, Britain had done its best to stop the mouths of generations of its tongue-tied citizens, America and France – that revolutionary junta – thereafter gave them voice. Moreover, where my informal experience with language in the United States was certainly refreshing – as if a burden had been lifted – my formal involvement with it, in terms of the academic study of linguistics, proved in a much broader sense to be liberating. For once, I was in the right place at the right time. The 1940s and 1950s had seen the fine pre-Chomskyean flowering in America of one of the major intellectual enterprises of the previous hundred years: the immensely fruitful co-operation between 'structuralist' concepts and procedures in the fields of linguistics and of anthropology. The connection between language and culture which this established, with its dawning recognition that way of speaking and way of life were in effect coterminous and inseparable, resulted in a decisive advance in our understanding of and purchase on the complex nature of the worlds that human beings create. Its grounding perception of language as an inward-looking system of self-validating structures had provided the means for many of the first sympathetic studies of native American or 'Indian' languages and ways of life which did not impose on them or judge them by warping European standards. The initial impulse for such work no doubt sprang from the zeal of Christian missionaries, avid to bring word of their English-speaking God to a host of potential converts. But its broader implications, not least for American, European, and particularly for British culture, could be judged, rightly it seemed to me, to be enormous.

If *Structuralism and Semiotics* has any originality – and as an introductory text it modestly aspired to have none – it lies in the suggestion that the origins of structuralism are to be found in the United States as much as in France: that the influence of American structural linguistics on French anthropologists such as Claude Lévi-Strauss was crucial to its development and thus, in my own experience, to a formative change in our ways of thinking about the world. When those ways of thinking came under sharp attack – as they did in the British academic world of the 1970s and 1980s – it was handy to be able to point out that, far from offering yet another instance of the clever pirouetting of irresponsible left-wing European intellectuals (the adjectives were interchangeable), structuralism's roots were also embedded deep in the soil of the great democratic republic across the Atlantic. Its citizens, it could be added, not only spoke our language. When it came to the push, during the war, they had probably also saved our bacon.

To some degree, as the above makes clear, the impact was personal and perhaps, as a result, it should be discounted. It is always difficult to distinguish the casual revelations of growing up from the disconcerting groundswells of history. However, in my own case, maybe the two had to some extent coincided. Having encountered the American brand of structuralism, I duly returned, unwittingly primed, to late nineteen-fifties Britain. There, as luck, and a certain amount of discreet lobbying would have it, I was appointed to a coveted post at the University of Wales in Cardiff.

It is often necessary to explain to non-British readers – and this is still lamentably so in the case of a number of British readers – that Cardiff is not in England. Of course, it lies close to the English border and manifests at first sight what appears to be a standard provincial Englishness.

Nonetheless, during the latter part of the twentieth century, the city gradually revealed itself to be interestingly, even disturbingly, non-English, with the result that it increasingly became an excellent vantage-point from which to observe what might be termed the 'edge' of Englishness. I'm referring of course to the frontiers of a specific culture or way of life, although history demonstrates that, for the Welsh, their neighbour's 'edge' has on occasion proved to be something that can also be felt as well as observed. To speak personally, my own perception of it served gradually to make evident something that for most English and many British people had hitherto been almost inconceivable as well as virtually invisible: the plain fact that Englishness had an edge; a limit, a frontier, a boundary, a terminus. It was not, therefore, universal, endless, transcendent, the way things were supposed to be. Nor could it, as a result, be a license or a template for correcting them until they were.

Needless to say, I was by no means the first British academic whom the revolutionary democracies of the United States and France had taught to perceive, albeit dimly, not only how cultures were constructed, but the means by which some of them sought to conceal their own constructedness under a cloak of inevitability. It is also unsurprising that such perceptions should present themselves in Britain at a time when, hindsight confirms, the fulcrum of English-speaking power in the world was shifting decisively from one side of the Atlantic to the other. Each of these factors contributed something to the atmosphere and the impulse that generated this volume, and indeed the New Accents series at large. But the subtle imperatives of a particular location, the disconcerting liminality of Cardiff itself, were also crucial.

As one of the first volumes in the series, Structuralism and Semiotics could in any case lay claim to a mildly subversive purpose. It had little concern with the then-dominant British notion that the purpose of criticism was to address the question of literary worth. It sought to evaluate and uphold no 'great tradition' of novels, plays, or poems. Its interest lay rather in the distinctive nature of the literary artefact and in the ways in which its 'literariness' might be described and accounted for. Perhaps, as a result, a number of early reviewers seemed anxious, less to read it than to cast around for rubber gloves and a waste-disposal unit. Their tone was often nervously jocose. Terms such as ostranenie and *bricolage*, names such as 'Shklovsky' and 'Todorov', provoked gales of brawny incomprehension. 'Common sense', a much-treasured item in the repertoire of academic hysteria, was increasingly evoked, appealed to, trundled out and creakingly flexed. Choruses of 'but surely this is all dealt with in *Biographia Literaria*?' trilled anxiously from Wine Manciple and Senior Fellow. Vicars from Swansea wrote darkly to university Principals. In an atmosphere of truculent bafflement, 'idiotics' was only one of a number of less than rapier-like coinages, jauntily paraded as part of what began to seem like a desperate project to submerge the whole enterprise in a welter of prophylactic giggling. For a while, structuralism virtually became the unacceptable face of a larger evil called 'theory', a weapon of mass destruction wielded, sagacious academic voices assured us, by malevolent forces plotting the end of civilisation as we knew it. There were rumours of favourable reviews ruthlessly suppressed by one leading literary journal. There were intemperate exchanges, to which I couldn't resist contributing, in another. Those were the days.

Just why the structuralist perception was felt to be so readily, so necessarily, dismissable was never satisfactorily explained. Did it have something to do with the fact that, springing from the broadly democratic backgrounds of France and America, it did not employ the notions of 'taste' and 'discrimination' as overt weapons of class warfare? After all, the principles of a method of analysis such as structuralism can be systematically set out, taught, and learned. That was – and is – the central assumption and *raison d'être* of this book. On the other hand, the cloudier refinements of appraisal and assessment could hardly, their purveyors in the United Kingdom seemed always anxious to demonstrate, be so readily transmitted. F. R. Leavis's worryingly prim model 'This – doesn't it? – bears such a relation to that; this kind of thing – don't you find it so? – wears better than that.' was all very well.[1] But in practice, the tweedy discussion of taste, even the brandishing of lengthy quotations in the name of discrimination, often seemed to decline – not without a certain relish – into bad-tempered hectoring, wholesale denunciation and bullying character-assassination. To a

[1] See F. R. Leavis, *The Common Pursuit* London: Chatto & Windus 1952, Harmondsworth: Penguin Books 1962, pp. 215, 211–22

degree, it seemed, taste and discrimination, even the commonly pursued 'true judgement', were things you either had or you hadn't: to those who lacked any or all of them, they looked almost like qualities you had to be born with.

The idea that access to important matters of common concern can legitimately be restricted on the basis of birth has always suited sections of British society rather well. Of course, I exaggerate. But in the 1960s and 1970s it was (and to some degree still is) the case that of the three main instruments of government in the British Isles, the Crown, the House of Lords, and the House of Commons, admittance to two was restricted, wholly or in part, to those who inherited such rights by blood. To some, the ultimate crystallisation of such a civilisation – its literature – could scarcely be held susceptible to examination in any potentially de-mystifying terms such as those which structuralism seemed determined to bring to bear. Had not the critical tradition extending from Coleridge to Matthew Arnold and through T. S. Eliot to F. R. Leavis spoken chillingly of the truly small number of those genuinely capable of appreciating great writing?: of the consequent need for an 'elect' or praetorian élite of 'aliens' to defend and preserve the culture such writing embodied; a select, priestly 'clerisy' who would act as its guardians and arrange its carefully filtered transmission? To the extent that structuralism, as the leading edge of 'theory', challenged all that, to the degree that it helped puncture the balloons of 'discrimination' and 'taste' by a pinpricking examination of the social and linguistic interests served by such fantasies, then, from a British standpoint at any rate, it looked suspiciously like evidence of a mutiny within the ranks.

Of course, experience of these matters in the United States was rather different. Whereas in Britain, structuralism seemed an initial step in a democratising process whereby literary texts might be reinserted into the culture and society from which a Romantic, high-falutin' sense of Art had prised them, critical theory on the other side of the Atlantic appeared to offer opportunity of another sort. As Geoffrey Hartman has recognised, it seemed capable of bankrolling not a return to Englishness, but an escape from it: the development of a truly American literary criticism. No longer need the trans-atlantic knee bend before a deadening 'Arnoldian Concordat', that confection of inherited tradition and canon assembled and insisted upon by critics from Coleridge on. As ever, ideas imported from France seemed at first to offer to Americans the heady prospect of freedom.[2]

That battle continues. Meanwhile, it would be foolish to deny that, as part of it, a rougher-hewn and more deeply-rooted American tradition has for some time taken another view, judging the development of literary theory, and in particular those who deal in it, to be committed to mystification of a different kind; one which actively diverts literature from its potentially liberating involvement with a general public and steers it into the stultifying embrace of professional academics – self-serving 'specialists' with their own careers to tend and a cash-crop of jargon to cultivate and harvest. Thus, paradoxically, what was enthusiastically greeted as 'left-wing' by some in Britain, has come in time to be no less forcefully derided as 'right-wing' by others in America. Yet even this offers, as no self-respecting theorist could resist pointing out, an excellent example of the fundamental structuralist principle outlined above.

This is not to deny a more general sense amongst literary critics on both sides of the Atlantic that in any case, for structuralism, the game is finally up. The oppositions which it discerned, and on which its most penetrating analyses depended, have, under the deconstructive onslaught of philosophers such as Jacques Derrida and others, come to appear less solid, scarcely certain, and decidedly unverifiable. Instead, they have started to look uncomfortably like the unconscious prejudices of a language and a way of life in search of order and stability in a world that can genuinely offer neither. Just as the poised and carefully balanced 'ambiguities' admired by a formalist New Criticism began, when more rigorously prosecuted by structuralist analysis, to shatter into the undecideable, contradictory elements of *aporia*, so the pursuit of all structures now seems a doomed chasing after permanency, little better than a kind of whistling in the dark, a desperate clutching at control whilst teetering on the brink of a void. It's a situation which, to be fair, Roland Barthes had himself appeared finally to recognise and, in

---

[2] See Geoffrey Hartman, *Criticism in the Wilderness* (New Haven and London, Yale University Press, 1980), pp. 1–15.

his most ambitious work S/Z, tried to contain by the imposition of his notorious five 'codes' (see above, pp. 94–99).

But of course the Derridean project of 'deconstruction' is bound, by definition, to prove uncontainable and it seems by now to have dealt structuralism a fatal, disintegrating blow. Yet, in its wake, what has come to be called 'post-structuralism' appears in the very manner of its self-announcement to be committed, willy-nilly, to a recognition of structuralism's role; awarding it, in that 'post', some sort of initiating, ground-breaking status. And if, in these fast-moving times, a book written more than twenty-five years ago can claim any continuing value, that of *Structuralism and Semiotics* perhaps lies in the record it offers of the first, tentative staking out of what can now be seen as a vitally fruitful terrain.

One of the most important insights achieved by the last century's combined projects of anthropology and linguistics was probably the recognition of structuralism's – and so 'theory's – ubiquity. Nobody just exists. If the distinctive human characteristic resides in our habitual involvement in 'ways of life' in terms of their constant making and re-making of apparent structures that cause the world to seem meaning-ful, then the capacity for that involvement derives from and depends upon an abstract 'theoretical' knowledge of how those structuring pro-cedures work. That knowledge, which usually operates outside of con-scious awareness, is something we all require in order to be able to live as members of a culture, and this remains so, regardless of whether such structures and structuring are logically sustainable by 'objective' stand-ards. If to be human is to belong to a way of life, then it is also to be a structuralist. And to be a structuralist is ultimately also to be a theorist. Attitudes to interpretation which grandly proclaim their holders to be theory-free, such as T. S. Eliot's 'there is no method except to be very intelligent' (see above, p. 126) can readily be persuaded to reveal their roots in complex if deliberately self-masking theories, not only of litera-ture, but of history and economics too. Irreverently probed by structur-alists and others, even the academic subject called 'English' will own up to its stake in the political programme it was invented to serve.

Structuralism's capacity to tease out such matters, its ability to 'x-ray' texts and cultures and to gain access, as a result, to whatever it is they hold in common, made it a powerful analytic tool. But does it still have anything to say, twenty-five years on, to the student of literature? In the strong belief that it does, and as a concluding example of the forceful insights it remains able to deploy, let me offer a slightly revised version of the four general maxims initially sketched out above (see pp. 127–28). Any student of literature would do well to ponder their implications:

1. There are no 'innocent' readers. We all confront texts partly or wholly in the grip of the structures bequeathed to us by our own culture, which we have no choice but to inherit. They form the basis of the economic, political, social and aesthetic presuppositions that make us what we are.

2. There are no 'objective' or 'transparent' texts. All texts, literary or otherwise, contain structuring features of language that relentlessly and unavoidably interpose themselves between the words on the page and whatever it is those words refer to. Rhymes, rhythms, assonances, alliterations, metaphors occur in all uses of language, not just those we think of as literary. They cannot be eradicated. In the end, they ensure that all texts draw attention in some degree to their own use of language, and thus to themselves, as well as to whatever they announce as their object.

3. There is no 'neutral' criticism. All critical stances betray some aspect or other of the political and ideological structures within which they are adopted, whether they support or aim to subvert, or even ignore them. Criticism comes from within a society, and that society's concerns cannot help but mark in some way the criticism it produces.

I still believe, unrepentantly, that precepts such as these can offer significant help in the negotiation of a number of the confusions that still swirl about literature and the relation of criticism to it. In fact, it now seems to me, turning these pages once more, that they lead inevitably, and as a bonus, to a fourth: one which I'm happy to propose as a kind of structuralist springboard into the future:

4. The text can't 'mean' by itself. It isn't a finished, ready-made product, with its meaning secreted inside it, like a stone in a

cherry, waiting to be plucked out. Any text only becomes meaningful when the reader works on it, by reading, and thus inserts it into a specific discursive structure responsive to the pressures – economic, political, historical – of a particular time and a particular place. Its meaning depends upon and derives from this process, and will change as the discourse into which it is inserted changes. This must mean that the reader is not the inert consumer of a pre-packaged text. The reader uses the text in order to produce meaning. In short, the *text* doesn't mean. The *reader* means *by* the text.

No doubt any claims I make for structuralism's ability to clarify, enlighten, and generally sweep away critical clutter should be set against the proliferating clouds of mystifying theoretical jargon that currently fog the pages of many a literary journal. But despite all the hand-wringing which that produces, we can no longer fail to recognise that the slogans it set out to replace, proposing 'the common pursuit of true judgement' or defending a 'great tradition', were themselves aspects of an older, and more pernicious – because vehemently denied – system of mystification: one which deployed not only jargon – often the peculiarly British sort that masquerades as plain speaking – but sackfuls of those deodorised and smoothed over presuppositions and prejudices from which we love to construct the 'self-evident'.

Inevitably, Chicken-Licken remains alive and well, his squawks defending a notion of art and of literature that will always claim to be able to soar beyond the reach of a material here, a concrete now and a critical analysis rooted in both. If structuralism did nothing else, it challenged, or offered the means to subvert those presumptions. It made the reader a discoverer, not of someone else's meaning, but of the basis of his or her own. It established the grounding principle, to paraphrase Roland Barthes (see above, p. 130), that if literature proposes, the reader disposes. The active, involving role this gives to the critic's voice is one which *Structuralism and Semiotics* energetically sought to foster. It still does.

So, looking back, I'm rather glad I didn't bother to do anything about my accent. As things turned out, it was much more useful to try to do something, if only a very little, about the context in which accents occur, and are perceived: factors which can make them sound, as a result, quite new. It is tempting to suggest that my fellow Midlander, that tortuously-vowelled, bald, bearded and beruffed playwright whose business was always the way people speak to each other, might even have approved.

Terence Hawkes
February, 2003

BIBLIOGRAPHY

(revised, 1983)

THE mass of writings on structuralism and semiotics is so vast that a simple alphabetical listing of material would not only lie beyond the scope of this book, but would also defeat its purpose. What follows is a selective list arranged under the following headings: I. Introductory material; II. Linguistics and Anthropology; III. Formalism; IV. Structuralism, texts and commentaries: (a) General, (b) Literary Criticism, (c) Other fields; V. Semiotics; VI. Some relevant journals. It is intended both to direct the beginning student towards the most helpful material in those areas covered by this book, and to suggest further reading for those who wish to move beyond its evident limitations. Some basic reading patterns in connection with particular topics are suggested at the end.

I. INTRODUCTORY MATERIAL, ANTHOLOGIES, COLLECTIONS OF ESSAYS

1. CAWS, PETER, 'What is Structuralism?', *Partisan Review*, Vol. 35, No. I, Winter 1968, pp. 75–91. Straightforward introductory essay.
2. DE GEORGE, RICHARD T. and FERNANDE M. (eds), *The Structuralists: from Marx to Lévi-Strauss* (New York: Doubleday, Anchor Books, 1972). A useful, if rather wide-ranging collection containing material by Marx, Freud, Saussure, Jakobson ('Closing statement: linguistics and poetics'), Lévi-Strauss (analysis, with Jakobson, of Baudelaire's

Les Chats), Barthes, ('The structuralist activity' and 'To write, an intransitive verb?') Althusser, Foucault, Lacan. Helpful overview offered in the introduction.

3. EHRMANN, JACQUES, (ed.), *Structuralism* (New York: Doubleday, Anchor Books, 1970). Reprint of a special issue of *Yale French Studies* (Nos. 36–7, 1966). Includes Lévi-Strauss, 'Overture' to *Le Cru et le cuit*, Michael Riffaterre on the Lévi-Strauss-Jakobson analysis of Baudelaire's *Les Chats*, and articles on structuralism in the fields of linguistics, anthropology, art, psychiatry and literature. Good bibliographies up to 1968.

4. JEFFERSON, ANN and ROBEY, DAVID (eds), *Modern Literary Theory: A Comparative Introduction* (London: Batsford, 1982). Contains lucid introductory essays by Ann Jefferson on Russian Formalism, structuralism and poststructuralism, together with valuable bibliographies.

5. LANE, MICHAEL (ed.), *Structuralism, A Reader* (London: Cape, 1970). Contains some valuable material: Barthes, 'Historical discourse', and 'Science versus literature'; Jakobson, 'On Russian fairy tales' as well as the Lévi-Strauss–Jakobson analysis of Baudelaire's *Les Chats*. Good bibliography.

6. PIAGET, JEAN, *Structuralism* (*Le Structuralisme*, Paris: P.U.F., 1968) translated and edited by Chaninah Maschler (London: Routledge & Kegan Paul, 1971). One of the central texts, valuable for its 'definitions' (chapter I) and for its discussion of structuralism in the field of mathematics, logic, biology, psychology, linguistics, philosophy and the social sciences. Fairly advanced.

7. ROBEY, DAVID (ed.), *Structuralism: An Introduction* (Oxford: Clarendon Press, 1973). Contains some helpful introductory pieces by Lyons, 'Structuralism and linguistics', Culler, 'The linguistic basis of structuralism', Leach, 'Structuralism in social anthropology', Eco, 'Social life as a sign system' and Todorov, 'The structural analysis of literature'.

8. STURROCK, JOHN (ed.), *Structuralism and Since: From Lévi-Strauss to Derrida* (Oxford: Oxford University Press, 1979). Valuable introductory essays by Sturrock (on Barthes), Dan Sperber (on Lévi-Strauss), Hayden White (on Foucault), Malcolm Bowie (on Lacan) and Jonathan Culler (on Derrida) which look beyond structuralism to poststructuralism.

9. WAHL, FRANÇOIS (ed.), *Qu'est-ce-que le structuralisme?* (Paris: Seuil, 1968). Wide-ranging collection of introductory essays, including

Todorov on 'Poetique' and Wahl on 'La philosophie entre l'avant et l'après du structuralisme'.

II. LINGUISTICS AND ANTHROPOLOGY

10. BENVENISTE, EMILE, *Problems in General Linguistics* (*Problèmes de linguistique générale*, Paris: Gallimard, 1966; Miami: University of Miami Press, 1971). His distinction between story (*l'histoire*) and discourse (*discours*) has proved fruitful. See Culler, *Structuralist Poetics*, pp. 197 ff. Advanced.

11. BLOOMFIELD, LEONARD, *Language* (London: Allen and Unwin, 1935). A classic of American 'structural' linguistics.

12. CARPENTER, EDMUND and MCLUHAN, MARSHALL, (eds), *Explorations in Communication* (Boston: Beacon Press, 1960). Contains valuable essays by Dorothy Lee, Carpenter, McLuhan and others.

13. CLUYSENAAR, ANNE, *Introduction to Literary Stylistics: A Discussion of Dominant Structures in Verse and Prose*, (London: Batsford, 1976).

14. FREEMAN, DONALD C. (ed.), *Linguistics and Literary Style* (New York and London: Holt, Rinehart and Winston, 1970). Interesting collection of essays, including Jan Mukařovský's 'Standard language and poetic language'.

15. FRIES, CHARLES C., *Linguistics and Reading* (New York and London: Holt, Rinehart and Winston, 1964). Chapter 2 'Linguistics: the study of language' offers a simple historical account of the subject's development: helps to establish bearings.

16. JAKOBSON, ROMAN, *Selected Writings* (4 vols.) (The Hague: Mouton, 1962–) Vol. I: *Phonological Studies*, 1962; Vol. II: *Word and Language*, 1971 (contains 'Language in relation to other communication systems' pp. 697–708, which maps the field of semiotics); Vol. III: *Poetry of Grammar and Grammar of Poetry* (forthcoming); Vol. IV *Slavic Epic Studies*, 1966.

17. —— *Questions de Poétique* (Paris: Seuil, 1973). Includes a French translation of 'Poetry of grammar and grammar of poetry' from *Lingua*, Vol. 21, 1968, pp. 597–609, and of *Shakespeare's Verbal Art in 'Th' Expence of Spirit* (with Lawrence Jones) The Hague: Mouton, 1970). Both these essays are worth looking at in either the English or the French version. In connection with the latter, see I. A. Richards 'Jakobson's Shakespeare: the subliminal structures of a sonnet', *The Times Literary Supplement*, 28 May 1970, pp. 589–96.

18. —— 'Closing statement: linguistics and poetics' One of Jakobson's

most influential essays: essential reading. See Sebeok (ed.) *Style in Language* (in this section).

19. —— and HALLE, MORRIS, *Fundamentals of Language* (Janua Linguarum, Series Minor, I, The Hague: Mouton, 1956). Part II, 'Two aspects of language and two types of aphasic disturbances' pp. 69–96, is by Jakobson, and expounds his crucial distinction between metaphor and metonymy.

20. —— see Culler, Jonathan 'Jakobson and the linguistic analysis of literary texts', *Language and Style*, Vol. V, No. I, Winter 1971, pp. 53–66.

21. —— see Erlich, Victor 'Roman Jakobson: grammar of poetry and poetry of grammar' in Chatman (ed.) *Approaches to Poetics* (see section IV).

22. LEACH, EDMUND, *Culture and Communication: the logic by which symbols are connected* (London: Cambridge University Press, 1976). Short, lucid and extremely helpful introduction to fundamental structuralist concepts in anthropology, which can profitably be read by anyone interested in any aspect of structuralism and semiotics. Designed for beginners. Good bibliography.

23. LEECH, G. N., *A Linguistic Guide to English Poetry* (London: Longman, 1969). Useful introduction.

24. LÉVI-STRAUSS, CLAUDE, *Tristes Tropiques* (Paris: Plon, 1955); translated and abridged, New York: Athenaeum, 1964; trans. John & Doreen Weightman (London: Cape, 1973; Penguin Books, 1976). Personal – and moving – account of his early anthropological work.

25. —— *Structural Anthropology* (*Anthropologie Structurale*, Paris: Plon, 1958); trans. Claire Jacobson and Brooke Grundfest Schoepf (London: Allen Lane, 1968; Penguin Books, 1972). Chapters II ('Structural analysis in linguistics and anthropology') and XI ('The structural study of myth') are particularly important.

26. —— *The Scope of Anthropology* (*Leçon inaugurale*, Collège de France, Paris: Gallimard, 1960); trans. Sherry Ortner Paul & Robert A. Paul (London: Cape, 1967).

27. —— *Totemism* (*Le Totémisme aujourd'hui*, Paris: P.U.F. 1962); trans. Rodney Needham, with an introduction by Roger C. Poole (Penguin Books, 1969). Poole's introduction is very helpful.

28. —— *The Savage Mind* (*La Pensée Sauvage*, Paris: Plon, 1962; London: Weidenfeld and Nicolson, 1966). An important work, with serious implications for the European mind.

29. —— *The Raw and the Cooked* (*Le Cru et le Cuit*, Paris: Plon, 1964);

trans. John & Doreen Weightman (London: Cape, 1970). This volume and the following one perhaps represent Lévi-Strauss's major achievement, as a professional anthropologist.

30. —— *From Honey to Ashes* (*Du Miel aux Cendres*, Paris: Plon, 1966); trans. John & Doreen Weightman (London: Cape, 1973).

31. —— 'The Story of Asdiwal' (*Le Geste d' Asdiwal*) in Edmund Leach (ed.), *The Structural Study of Myth and Totemism* (London: Tavistock, 1967) pp. 1–47. A fine example of 'structural' anthropology in action. The same volume contains critical commentaries on Lévi-Strauss by Mary Douglas, Nur Yalman and K. O. L. Burridge.

32. —— with Charbonnier, G., *Conversations with Claude Lévi-Strauss*, trans. John and Doreen Weightman (London, Cape, 1969). Transcriptions of broadcasts. 'Conversation' covers art, poetry, music, language.

33. —— See Steiner, George 'Orpheus with his myths: Claude Lévi-Strauss' in *Language and Silence* (London: Faber, 1967; Penguin Books 1969, pp. 248–60).

34. —— see Hayes, E. Nelson and Tanya (eds), *Claude Lévi-Strauss: The Anthropologist as Hero* (Cambridge, Mass.: M.I.T. Press, 1970). Interesting, with extensive bibliography.

35. —— see Leach, Edmund, *Claude Lévi-Strauss* (London: Fontana, 1970). Probably the best 'basic' introduction.

36. —— see Paz, Octavio, *Claude Lévi-Strauss: An Introduction* (London: Cape, 1970).

37. LEVIN, SAMUEL R., *Linguistic Structures in Poetry* (The Hague: Mouton, 1962) Janua Linguarum Series No. 23.

38. —— 'The conventions of poetry' see Chatman (ed.), *Literary Style: A Symposium* in section IV.

39. MINNIS, NOEL (ed.), *Linguistics at Large* (London: Paladin, 1973). Fourteen lectures given at the Institute of Contemporary Arts, London 1969–70. Interesting material by R. H. Robins, 'The structure of language', George Steiner, 'Linguistics and literature' and Edmund Leach, 'Language and anthropology' among others.

40. MUKAŘOVSKÝ, jan, 'Standard language and poetic language', an important essay reprinted in the following anthologies listed in this bibliography: (ed.) Freeman (this section); Garvin (section III); Chatman and Levin (section IVb). His essay 'The esthetics of language' in the Garvin vol. is also of interest.

41. PIKE, KENNETH L., *Language in Relation to a Unified Theory of Human Behaviour* (The Hague: Mouton, 1966).

42. SAPIR, EDWARD, *Language* (New York: Harcourt Brace, 1921).

43. ——— *Selected Writings in Language Culture and Personality*, ed. David G. Mandelbaum (Berkeley: University of California Press, 1949). Classic works by an early American structural linguist. See especially the essay 'The status of linguistics as a science' in the latter volume.

44. SAUSSURE, FERDINAND DE, *Course in General Linguistics* (*Cours de Linguistique Générale* ed. Charles Bally, Albert Sechehaye with Albert Riedlinger, 1915); trans. Wade Baskin (New York: The Philosophical Library Inc. 1959; New York: McGraw Hill, 1966; London: Peter Owen, 1960; London: Fontana, 1974).

45. ——— See Culler, Jonathan, *Saussure* (London: Fontana, 1976). Valuable introduction, marking Saussure's elevation to the status of 'modern master'.

46. ——— see STAROBINSKI, JEAN, *Les Mots sur les Mots: Les anagrammes de Ferdinand de Saussure* (Paris: Gallimard, 1971). An account of Saussure's latter-day interest in one aspect of literary structuralism: anagrams.

47. SEBEOK, THOMAS A. (ed.), *Style in Language* (Cambridge, Mass.: M.I.T. Press, 1960). Seminal collection of essays, 'abstracts' and comments deriving from a 1958 conference of linguists, psychologists and literary critics. Of particular importance is Roman Jakobson's influential 'Closing statement: linguistics and poetics' pp. 350–77 which has become a standard point of reference for recent work in the field.

48. ——— A. (ed.), *Linguistics and Adjacent Arts and Sciences* (The Hague: Mouton, 1973). This is volume 12 of the *Current Trends In Linguistics* series, edited by Sebeok. In 3 Tomes, this survey contains sections on Semiotics (Part Two: it includes Sebeok's 'Semiotics: a survey of the state of the art') and Linguistics and the verbal arts (Part Three). The latter offers useful contributions from Frantisek Suejkovsky 'History of modern poetics', Pierre Guiraud 'Rhetoric and stylistics' and Tzvetan Todorov, 'Literary genres'.

49. TRAGER, GEORGE L. and SMITH, HENRY LEE JR, *An Outline of English Structure* (Washington: American Council of Learned Societies, 1951). An influential example of American structural linguistics.

50. VICO, GIAMBATTISTA, *The New Science*, a revised translation of the third edn by Thomas Goddard Bergin and Max Harold Fisch (Ithaca and London: Cornell University Press, 1968). See above pp. 11–15.

51. WHORF, BENJAMIN LEE, *Language, Thought and Reality*, ed. John B. Carroll (Cambridge, Mass.: M.I.T. Press, 1956). Key texts in the devel-

opment of the notion of cultural 'relativity', and of the anaesthetic domination of the structure of a language over 'reality'. An excellent account and assessment of the work of Whorf and Sapir in this field will be found in George Steiner's *After Babel: Aspects of Language and Translation* (London: Oxford University Press, 1975) pp. 87–94.

III. FORMALISM

52. BENNETT, TONY, *Formalism and Marxism* (London: Methuen, 1979).

53. ERLICH, VICTOR, *Russian Formalism: History-Doctrine* (The Hague: Mouton 1955, revised edn 1965). The fundamental introductory work.

54. —— 'Russian Formalism', *Journal of the History of Ideas*, October–December 1973, Vol. 34, No. 4, pp. 627–38.

55. GARVIN, PAUL L. (ed. and trans.), *A Prague School Reader on Aesthetics, Literary Structure and Style* (Washington DC: Georgetown University Press, 1964). Contains Mukařovský's 'Standard language and poetic language'.

56. HARTMAN, GEOFFREY, *Beyond Formalism* (New Haven and London: Yale University Press, 1970).

57. JAMESON, FREDRIC, *The Prison-House of Language: A Critical Account of Structuralism and Russian Formalism* (Princeton and London: Princeton University Press, 1972). A key work which makes an incisive critical analysis of the presuppositions of formalism and structuralism and offers a discriminating commentary on each. Necessary reading for advanced students.

58. —— *Marxism and Form* (Princeton and London: Princeton University Press, 1971). An assessment of Marxist critical theory against the background of formalism. Jameson presents a carefully argued case for a new 'dialectical' criticism, aware of structuralist and Marxist implications, and capable of undermining the illusions deriving from commitment to mere content of the work of art characteristic of much contemporary criticism. An important book, for advanced work.

59. JEFFERSON, ANN, see 4 above.

60. LEMON, LEE T. and REIS, MARION J. (eds and trans.), *Russian Formalist Criticism: Four Essays* (Lincoln: University of Nebraska Press, 1965). Useful introduction, plus essays by Shklovsky, 'Art as technique' and 'Sterne's *Tristram Shandy*', Tomashevsky, 'Thematics' and Eichenbaum, 'The theory of the formal method'.

61. MATEJKA, LADISLAV and POMORSKA, KRYSTYNA (eds), *Readings in*

Russian Poetics: Formalist and Structuralist Views (Cambridge, Mass.: M.I.T. Press, 1971). More extensive collection than Lemon and Reis, but also more expensive. Includes Eichenbaum's 'The theory of the formal method' in a different translation, and his essay on 'O. Henry and the theory of the short story', as well as work by Jakobson, Tomashevsky, Tynjanov, Brik, Shklovsky and others.

62. PROPP, V. I., *Morphology of the Folktale* (Leningrad 1928) trans. Laurence Scott, with an introduction by Svatava Pirkova-Jakobson (Austin and London: University of Texas Press, 1958; second edition revised and ed. by Louis A. Wagner, with an introduction by Alan Dundes, 1968). A basic text. See Hendricks in section IVb.

63. SHKLOVSKY, VIKTOR, *A Sentimental Journey: Memoirs 1917–1922* trans. Richard Sheldon (Ithaca and London: Cornell University Press, 1970). Fascinating account of his exile and the 'anarchy of life' by a leading spokesman of formalism.

64. —— *Zoo: or letters not about love* (1923) trans. Richard Sheldon (Ithaca and London: Cornell University Press, 1971). An experimental novel that engagingly embodies some of Shklovsky's formalist theories.

65. TODOROV, TZVETAN (ed.), *Théorie de la littérature: textes des formalists russes* (Paris: Seuil, 1965). Selections from Russian formalists translated into French. An important collection, much of whose material is now available in English in the volumes edited by Lemon and Reis and by Matejka and Pomorska mentioned above.

66. WELLEK, RENÉ, *The Literary Theory and Aesthetics of the Prague School* (Ann Arbor: University of Michigan Press, 1969).

See also under *Twentieth Century Studies* in section VI.

IV. STRUCTURALISM: TEXTS AND COMMENTARIES

(a) General

67. BENOIST, JEAN-MARIE, *La révolution structurale* (Paris: Grasset, 1976). Comprehensive and critical review of recent developments in structuralist research. Advanced.

68. BOUDON, RAYMOND, *The Uses of Structuralism* (*A Quoi Sert La Notion de Structure*, Paris: Gallimard, 1968) trans. Michalina Vaughan (London: Heinemann, 1971). Rather abstract critical account of the concept of structure. Advanced.

69. FOUCAULT, MICHEL, *The Order of Things: an archaeology of the human sciences* (*Les mots et les choses*, Paris: Gallimard, 1966; London: Tavistock, 1970).

70. —— *The Archaeology of Knowledge* (*L'Archéologie du Savoir*, Paris: Gallimard, 1969; trans. A. M. Sheridan Smith, London: Tavistock, 1972). Foucault is a structuralist 'historian' of knowledge who argues among other things for the 'recent invention' of the idea of Man.

71. GARDNER, HOWARD, *The Quest for Mind: Piaget, Lévi-Strauss and the Structuralist Movement* (New York: Knopf, 1973).

72. MACKSEY, RICHARD and DONATO, EUGENIO (eds), *The Structuralist Controversy: The Languages of Criticism and the Sciences of Man* (Baltimore and London: Johns Hopkins University Press, 1970 and 1972). Papers and discussions from an internal symposium on 'The languages of criticism and the sciences of Man' held at Johns Hopkins in 1966. A seminal collection, containing material from most of the major structuralists: Goldmann, Todorov ('Language and literature') Barthes ('To Write: an intransitive verb') Lacan, Derrida ('Structure, sign and play in the discourse of the human sciences'). Valuable for advanced work.

73. PETTIT, PHILIP, *The Concept of Structuralism* (London: Gill and Macmillan, 1976). Philosophical analysis of structuralism's premises.

(b) Structuralism and literary criticism

74. BARTHES, ROLAND, *Writing Degree Zero* (*Le Degré Zéro de L'Ecriture*, Paris: Seuil, 1953); trans. Annette Lavers and Colin Smith (London: Cape, 1967). See above pp. 107–10.

75. —— *On Racine* (*Sur Racine*, Paris: Seuil, 1963); trans. Richard Howard (New York: Hill and Wang, 1964).

76. —— *Critical Essays* (*Essais Critiques*, Paris: Seuil, 1964); trans. Richard Howard (Evanston, Ill.: North-western University Press, 1972).

77. —— *Critique et vérité* (Paris: Seuil, 1966).

78. —— *S/Z* (Paris: Seuil, 1970), trans. Richard Miller, with a preface by Richard Howard (London: Cape, 1975). Possibly Barthes's most brilliant work (see above pp. 114 ff). An exhilarating analysis, but not as original as some of his commentators suggest. His five 'codes' of meaning should be compared, as a *modus operandi*, with Empson's seven 'types' of ambiguity: see below, this section.

79. —— *The Pleasure of the Text* (*Le Plaisir du Texte*, Paris: Seuil, 1975);

trans. Richard Miller, with a note on the text by Richard Howard (London: Cape, 1976). See above, p. 115.

80. —— 'Introduction à l'analyse structurale des récits' see under *Communications* and *Working Papers in Cultural Studies* in section VI.

81. —— 'Science versus literature', *The Times Literary Supplement*, 28th September 1967, pp. 897–8. See also Lane (ed.) in section I.

82. —— 'Style and its image', see Chatman (ed.) this section and *Communications* and *Working Papers in Cultural Studies*, section VI.

83. —— 'To write, an intransitive verb' see De George R. T. and F. M. (eds) in section I and Macksey and Donato (eds) in section IV (a).

84. —— see Jonathan Culler, *Barthes* (London: Fontana 1983). The best short introduction: lucid, condensed, accurate.

85. —— see Annette Lavers, *Roland Barthes, Structuralism and After* (London: Methuen, 1982). The best full introduction: complex, demanding, accurate.

86. —— see Philip Thody, *Roland Barthes, A Conservative Estimate* (London: Macmillan, 1977). Oversimplifying anglicization; very conservative.

87. —— see John Sturrock, 'Roland Barthes – a profile', *The New Review* Vol. I, No. 2, May 1974, pp. 13–21.

For further works by Barthes see section V.

88. CHATMAN, SEYMOUR (ed.), *Literary Style: A symposium* (London: Oxford University Press, 1971). A valuable collection which includes Barthes, 'Style and its image', Todorov, 'The place of style in the structure of the text', Wellek, 'Stylistics, poetics and criticism' and Samuel R. Levin, 'The conventions of poetry' among others.

89. —— (ed.), *Approaches to Poetics* (New York and London: Columbia University Press, 1973). Includes Victor Erlich, 'Roman Jakobson: grammar of poetry and poetry of grammar' – a valuable survey and critique of Jakobson's work, together with essays by Frank Kermode, Richard Ohmann, Stanley Fish, Todorov and others.

90. —— 'New ways of analyzing narrative structure', *Language and Style*, Vol. 2, No. I, 1969, pp. 3–36. Deals with Propp, Barthes, Todorov, and analyses Joyce's 'Eveline'.

91. —— and LEVIN, SAMUEL R. (eds), *Essays on the Language of Literature* (Boston: Houghton Mifflin, 1967). Contains Mukařovský's 'Standard Language and Poetic Language' as well as essays by Jakobson and Halliday.

92. CULLER, JONATHAN, *Structuralist Poetics: structuralism, linguistics and the study of literature* (London: Routledge and Kegan Paul, 1975).

Convincing argument for a new direction in structuralist criticism, which also provides an informative introduction to the field. Excellent bibliography. See above, pp. 158–60.

93. DOUBROVSKY, SERGE, *The New Criticism in France (Pourquoi la nouvelle critique?*, Paris: Mercure de France, 1966); trans. Derek Coltman, with an introduction by Edward Wasiolek (Chicago and London: University of Chicago Press, 1973). A good account of the issues at stake in the Picard-Barthes debate, with their implications for literary criticism at large. Wasiolek's introduction offers a judicious assessment of the arguments as they affect American 'New Criticism', and has an excellent bibliography of Barthes, New Criticism and Russian Formalism.

94. EMPSON, WILLIAM, *Seven Types of Ambiguity (London*: Chatto, 1930, 1947; Penguin Books, 1961). Once considered a classic of 'New Criticism', this is a work which structuralists continue to find fascinating, and have begun to claim for their own persuasion. It bears comparison with Barthes's *S/Z* and is a key text in the development of modern critical consciousness.

95. FORREST-THOMSON, VERONICA, 'Necessary artifice: form and theory in the poetry of *Tel Quel'*, *Language and Style*, Vol. VI, No. I, 1973, pp. 3–26.

96. FRYE, NORTHROP, *Anatomy of Criticism* (Princeton and London: Princeton University Press, 1957). A classic of North American structuralism.

97. GENETTE, GÉRARD, *Figures I* (Paris: Seuil, 1966), *Figures II*, 1969, *Figures III*, 1972. Untreated in the present volume, Genette is an important figure in literary structuralism. See Culler, pp. 102 ff.

98. —— *Mimologiques* (Paris: Seuil, 1976). Words as 'mimics' of the structures of reality.

99. GOLDMANN, LUCIEN, *The Hidden God (Le Dieu Caché*, Paris: Gallimard, 1959; London: Routledge and Kegan Paul, 1964).

100. —— *Pour une sociologie du roman* (Paris: Gallimard, 1964). Goldmann develops an approach which combines Marxism and structuralism. See Jameson, section III.

101. GREIMAS, A. J., *Sémantique Structurale* (Paris: Larousse, 1966).

101. —— *Du Sens* (Paris: Seuil, 1970). See above pp. 87 ff. For further works of Greimas see section V.

103. GUILLÉN, CLAUDIO, *Literature as System* (Princeton and London: Princeton University Press, 1971).

104. HEATH, STEPHEN, *The Nouveau Roman: a Study in the Practice of*

Writing (London: Elek, 1972). The first chapter contains one of the best accounts of the 'structuralist' view of the novel. See also his 'Towards textual semiotics' in *Signs of the Times*, under Heath *et al.* (eds), in section V.

105. HENDRICKS, WILLIAM O., 'Folklore and the structural analysis of literary texts', *Language and Style*, Vol. III, No. 2, 1970, pp. 83–121. Deals with Propp and others.

106. HILL, ARCHIBALD A., 'An analysis of *The Windhover*: an experiment in structural method', *PMLA* Vol. LXX, No. 5, December 1955, pp. 968–78. A good example of 'early' American structural criticism, deriving from structural linguistics.

107. JAMESON, FREDRIC, *The Prison House of Language* and *Marxism and Form*. Both these works focus on literary criticism: see section III.

108. JOSIPOVICI, GABRIEL, *The World and the Book* (London: Macmillan, 1971). Chapter 2, 'Surfaces and structures' gives a clear account of the issues in the Picard-Barthes debate. Cf. Doubrovsky, this section.

109. KERMODE, FRANK, *The Sense of an Ending: Studies in the Theory of Fiction* (New York: Oxford University Press, 1967). Not a work of structuralist criticism, but Chapter 5 'Literary fiction and reality' raises important issues.

110. LENTRICCHIA, FRANK, *After The New Criticism* (Chicago: University of Chicago Press, London: Athlone Press, 1980; Methuen, 1983). Chapter 4 is on Structuralism; Chapter 5 is on Poststructuralism. Advanced.

111. LODGE, DAVID, *The Modes of Modern Writing* (London: Arnold, 1977, 1979). A sustained and largely successful attempt to apply Jakobson's categories to Joyce, Stein, Hemingway, Lawrence, Woolf and others. Lucid introduction to Jakobson.

112. —— *Working With Structuralism* (London: Routledge and Kegan Paul, 1981). A collection of essays rather loosely focused on the application of structuralism to a variety of literary topics.

113. MAGLIOLA, ROBERT, 'Parisian Structuralism confronts Phenomenology: the ongoing debate', *Language and Style*, Vol. VI, No. 4, Fall 1973, pp. 237–48. A good survey of the scene.

114. NIEL, A., *L'analyse structurale des textes* (Paris: Mame, 1973).

115. PICARD, RAYMOND, *Nouvelle critique ou nouvelle imposture?* (Paris: Pauvert, 1965). See Doubrovsky and Josipovici this section, also above p. 111 ff.

116. SCHOLES, ROBERT, *Structuralism in Literature: An Introduction* (New Haven and London: Yale University Press, 1974). The first book-length introductory survey in English: useful bibliography.

117. TODOROV, TZVETAN, *Grammaire du Décaméron* (The Hague: Mouton, 1969) see under Sebeok (ed.) *Approaches to Semiotics* in section V.

118. —— *Littérature et signification* (Paris: Larousse, 1967). A structural analysis of *Les Liaisons Dangereuses*.

119. —— *Poétique de la Prose* Paris: Seuil, 1971). Essays on the theory of fiction.

120. —— *Introduction à la littérature fantastique* (Paris: Seuil, 1970; translated by Richard Howard, Cleveland: Case Western Reserve University Press, 1973). Todorov is a prolific writer, and pieces by him will be found under various headings elsewhere in this bibliography. See Robey (ed.) and Wahl (ed.) in section I; Macksey and Donato (eds) in section IV (a); Chatman (ed.) in section IV(b); Sebeok (ed.) in section V; and under *Communications, Poetics, Screen, Twentieth Century Studies, The Times Literary Supplement* and *Yale French Studies* in section VI. See also the extensive bibliography in Culler's *Structuralist Poetics*, and Scholes's *Structuralism in Literature*.

121. WATSON, GEORGE, 'Old furniture and "nouvelle critique" ', *Encounter*, February, 1975, pp. 43–54. Vigorous attack on structuralist criticism and its 'nationalistic' character: 'Its object is to allow a sense of national grandeur to survive untouched.'

122. WELLEK, RENÉ and WARREN, AUSTIN, *Theory of Literature* (2nd edn, London: Cape, 1954; 3rd edn, Penguin Books, 1963). Places structuralism in a wider context.

123. WELLEK, RENÉ, *Concepts of Criticism* (New Haven and London: Yale University Press, 1963). The essay on 'The revolt against positivism in recent European literary scholarship' is rewarding.

(c) Structuralism and other fields

124. GLUCKSMANN, MIRIAM, *Structuralist Analysis in Contemporary Social Thought* (London: Routledge and Kegan Paul, 1974). Compares Lévi-Strauss and Althusser.

125. LACAN, JACQUES, *The Language of the Self: The Function of Language in Psychoanalysis*, with an introduction by Anthony Wilden (Baltimore and London: Johns Hopkins University Press, 1968). A controversial structuralist approach to psychoanalysis and language. See Lacan's contributions to De George (eds) and Ehrmann (ed.) in section I and to Macksey and Donato (eds) in section IV (a). Wilden's introduction is complex but rewarding.

126. METZ, CHRISTIAN, *Film Language* (London: Oxford University Press, 1974).

127. ——— *Language and Cinema* (The Hague: Mouton, 1974) see under Sebeok (ed.) *Approaches to Semiotics*, section V. Metz is the foremost structuralist (or 'semioticist') analyst of film, and his books must be regarded as basic texts in this field. See the special issue of *Screen* mentioned in section VI.

V. SEMIOTICS

128. BARTHES ROLAND, *Mythologies* (a selection from *Mythologies*, Paris: Seuil, 1957); trans. Annette Lavers (London: Cape, 1972; Paladin, 1973). A series of incisive and often amusing short studies of contemporary 'myths', followed by one of the fundamental texts of modern semiotic theory; 'Myth today'.

129. ——— *Elements of Semiology* (*Eléments de Sémiologie*, Paris: Seuil, 1964); trans. Annette Lavers and Colin Smith (London: Cape, 1967). See above, pp. 133 ff. Another fundamental text. Rather abstract: it helps to read 'Myth today' first.

130. ——— *Système de la Mode* (Paris: Seuil, 1967). The semiotics of fashion-writing.

131. ——— 'La linguistique du discours'. See Greimas (ed.) *Sign, Language, Culture*, this section.

132. ——— 'Rhetoric of the image' ('Rhetorique de l'image') see *Communications* and *Working Papers in Cultural Studies* in section VI.

133. BIRDWHISTELL, RAY L., *Kinesics and Context* (London: Allen Lane, The Penguin Press, 1971). Classic essays on bodily communication.

134. COQUET, JEAN-CLAUDE, *Semiotique Littéraire* (Paris: Mame, 1973).

135. ——— and KRISTEVA, JULIA, 'Sémanalyse: conditions d'une sémiotique scientifique', *Semiotica* No. 5, 1972, pp. 324–49.

136. CORTI, MARIA, *An Introduction to Literary Semiotics* (Bloomington: Indiana University Press, 1978).

137. CULLER, JONATHAN, *The Pursuit of Signs* (London: Routledge and Kegan Paul, 1981). A wide-ranging collection of essays which offers an over-view of the contribution of semiotics to literary criticism as well as more specific studies.

138. DERRIDA, JACQUES, *De La Grammatologie* (Paris: Minuit, 1967).

139. ——— *L'Ecriture et la différence* (Paris: Seuil, 1967). See above pp. 145 ff.

140. ——— 'Sémiologie et grammatologie', *Social Science Information*, Vol. 7, No. 3, 1968, pp. 135–48.

141. —— 'The ends of man', *Philosophy and Phenomenological Research*, Vol. XXX, 1969–70, pp. 31–57.

142. ECO, UMBERTO, *A Theory of Semiotics* (Bloomington and London: Indiana University Press, 1976). A re-working and revision by the author, in English, of previous work, including *La struttura assente* (Milan: Bompiani, 1968), and *Le forme del contenuto* (Milan: Bompiani, 1971). A formidable attempt at a unified theory: not for beginners, but valuable to work through.

143. —— *The Role of the Reader: Explorations in the Semiotics of Texts* (Bloomington: Indiana University Press, 1979). Nine essays on diverse subjects ranging from metaphor to Superman.

144. —— and DEL BUONO, E., *The Bond Affair* (London: Macdonald, 1966). Interesting analyses of the James Bond novels, including Eco's 'Narrative Structure in Fleming' pp. 37–75, developed from his article 'James Bond: une combinatoire narrative', *Communications* No. 8, 1966: see section VI.

145. ELAM, KEIR, *The Semiotics of Theatre and Drama* (London: Methuen, 1980).

146. GREIMAS, A. J. (ed.), *Sign, Language, Culture* (The Hague: Mouton, 1970). Includes Barthes's 'La linguistique du discours', and sections on 'The semiotics of film' and 'The semiotics of literature' among many others.

147. —— (ed.), *Essais de Sémiotique Poétique* (Paris: Larousse, 1971). Includes work by Kristeva on Mallarmé as well as Greimas's interesting essay 'Pour une théorie du discours poétique.'

148. GUIRAUD, PIERRE, *Semiology* (*La Sémiologie*, Paris: P.U.F. 1971); trans. George Gross (London: Routledge and Kegan Paul, 1975). Somewhat compressed account of general principles, but offers a valuable survey of the field.

149. HALL, EDWARD T., *The Silent Language* (New York: Doubleday, 1959). Classic account of non-verbal communication as a part of culture.

150. HEATH, STEPHEN, MCCABE, COLIN and PRENDERGAST, C. (eds), *Signs of the Times* (Cambridge: Granta, 1971). Interesting collection of essays, somewhat difficult to obtain. Includes 'A conversation with Roland Barthes', Heath's 'Towards textual semiotics' and Kristeva's 'The semiotic activity'.

151. HERVEY, SANDOR, *Semiotic Perspectives* (London, Allen and Unwin, 1982). Thoroughgoing account of the whole field of semiotics: especially valuable distinction between Saussure and Peirce. Advanced.

152. HINDE, R. A., *Non-verbal communication* (Cambridge: Cambridge University Press, 1972).

153. JAKOBSON, ROMAN, *Coup de l'oeil sur le developpement de la sémiotique* (Studies in Semiotics 3, Research Center for Language and Semiotic Studies, Bloomington, Indiana, 1975).

154. —— 'Language in relation to other communication systems', *Selected Writings* Vol. II (The Hague: Mouton, 1971), pp. 697–708. Maps the whole field of semiotics.

155. KRISTEVA, JULIA, *Sémiotiké: Recherches pour une sémanalyse* (Paris: Seuil, 1969). A collection of previously published essays by a key member of the radical *Tel Quel* group.

156. —— *Le Texte du Roman* (The Hague: Mouton, 1971) an 'approche semiologique'. See Sebeok (ed.) this section.

157. —— *La révolution du langage poétique* (Paris: Seuil, 1974).

158. —— 'The semiotic activity' see under Heath *et al.* (eds) this section, and under *Screen* in section VI.

159. —— 'The system and the speaking subject' see under *The Times Literary Supplement* in section VI.

160. —— with REY-DEBOVE, J., and UMIKER, D.J. (eds), *Essays in Semiotics* (The Hague: Mouton, 1971). See Sebeok (ed.) this section.

161. MORRIS, CHARLES, *Writings on the General Theory of Signs* (The Hague: Mouton, 1971). A valuable collection of work by one of the most influential American semioticians. See Sebeok (ed.) this section.

162. PEIRCE, CHARLES SANDERS, *Collected Papers* (8 vols.) ed. Charles Hartshorne, Paul Weiss and Arthur W. Burks (Cambridge, Mass.: Harvard University Press, 1931–58). One of the two (with Saussure) founding fathers of modern semiotic studies, Peirce's writings are central and crucial to any advanced work in the field. A comprehensive 15 volume edition of Peirce's works, edited by Max H. Fisch and Edward C. Moore, is in preparation. When it appears it will constitute the first publication of much of his writing, and will enable a broader acknowledgement of its worth to be made.

163. REWAR, WALTER, 'Semiotics and communication in Soviet criticism', *Language and Style*, Vol. IX, No. I, Winter 1976, pp. 55–69. Surveys some recent work.

164. RIFFATERRE, MICHAEL, *Semiotics of Poetry* (Bloomington: Indiana University Press, 1978; London: Methuen, 1980). Interesting original statement by a major critic.

165. SCHOLES, ROBERT, *Semiotics and Interpretation* (New Haven and London: Yale University Press, 1982). Ebullient collection of essays

intended as a companion to the author's *Structuralism in Literature* (116 above). Provocative and informative.

166. SEBEOK, THOMAS A. (ed.), *Approaches to Semiotics* (The Hague: Mouton, 1969–). A series of books (including a paperback 'sub-series') dealing with a wide variety of contributions to the theory of signs. Includes Harley C. Shand's *Semiotic Approaches to Psychiatry* (Vol. 2, 1970) as well as Todorov's *Grammaire du Décaméron* (Vol. 3, 1969) and the volume ed. Kristeva, Rey-Debove and Umiker, *Essays in Semiotics* (Vol. 4, 1971) listed above. This is a massive collection, in English and French, of articles reprinted from the journal *Social Science Information*, and includes contributions from Kristeva, Derrida, Rulon Wells, Guiraud, Chatman and others, as well as a 'Bibliographie sémiotique 1964–5' by Todorov *et al.* Further volumes in the series include Kristeva's *Le Texte du Roman* (Vol. 6, 1971), the works by Charles Morris and Christian Metz listed above, and Segre's *Semiotics and Literary Criticism* (Vol. 35, 1973) listed below. Many other volumes are in preparation.

167. SEGRE, CESARE, *Semiotics and Literary Criticism* (*I Segni e la Critica*, Torino Einaudi: 1969) trans. John Meddemmen (The Hague: Mouton, 1973).

168. TODOROV, TZVETAN, 'Perspectives sémiologiques', *Communications* No. 7, 1966, pp. 139–45.

VI. SOME RELEVANT JOURNALS

169. *Bulletin of Literary Semiotics* (*BLS*) ed. Daniel Laferrière, Dept. of German and Russian, Tufts University, Medford, Mass., USA. An international 'newsletter' designed to inform about work in progress, conferences, publications, etc. Its first issue appeared in May 1975 and included a bibliography of recent work. The second issue (September 1975) contains a valuable history and survey of the field by Sebeok: 'The semiotic web: a chronicle of prejudices'.

170. *Communications* (published by the École Pratique des Hautes Études, Paris) has produced some of the most influential work in the field of structuralism. No. 8 (1966) is devoted wholly to the structural analysis of the text (*récit*) and contains some important statements, particularly Barthes's 'Introduction à l'analyse structurale des récits' and Todorov's 'Les catégories du récit littéraire'. Barthes's 'Rhetorique de l'image' appears in No. 4 (1964) and Todorov's 'Perspectives sémiologiques' appears in No. 7 (1966).

171. *Language and Style* ed. E. L. Epstein, Dept of English, Queens College, City University of New York, Flushing, New York, USA. Publishes material on all aspects of stylistics, including semiotics.

172. *Poetics*, published by Mouton, The Hague, since 1971. Contains structuralist analyses.

173. *Poetics Today* published by the Institute of Poetics and Semiotics, Tel Aviv University, Israel. Deals with all aspects of poetics, particularly descriptive poetics and semiotics. The Institute also publishes a series of 'Papers in Poetics and Semiotics'.

174. *Poétique*, published by Seuil, Paris. Edited by Genette and Todorov, publishes structuralist analyses.

175. *Screen* (The Journal of the Society for Education in Film and Television) has published a special double issue (Vol. 14, Nos 1 & 2, Spring/Summer 1973) devoted to 'Cinema semiotics and the work of Christian Metz'. Includes valuable reprints of essays by Todorov ('Semiotics'), Kristeva ('The semiotic activity') together with pieces by Metz, Heath and others. Good bibliography.

176. *Semiotica*, Journal of the International Association for Semiotic Studies (IASS). Ed. Sebeok, published by Mouton.

177. *Tel Quel*, published by Seuil, Paris. The most radical of the journals associated with structuralism and semiotics. Under the direction of a committee, it pursues 'une théorie et une pratique révolutionnaires de l'ecriture' through focusing on new forms of fiction, philosophy, science, and political analysis. Cf. Veronica Forrest-Thomson in section IV(b). A collection of essays by writers associated with the journal was published as *Théorie d'Ensemble* (Paris: Seuil, 1968). It contains work by Barthes, Derrida, Philippe Sollers, Kristeva, Foucault and others.

178. *The Times Literary Supplement* has devoted two special issues to semiotics under the title 'The Tell-Tale Sign' on 5 and 12 October 1973. These contain particularly interesting essays by Todorov ('Artistic language and ordinary language'), Tullio de Mauro ('The link with linguistics'), Eco ('Looking for a logic of culture') (5 October), and by Kristeva ('The system and the speaking subject') and Stephen Ullmann ('Natural and conventional Signs') (12 October). The essays have been revised and collected in *The Tell-Tale Sign: A Survey of Semiotics* ed. Sebeok, Lisse: Peter de Ridder Press, 1975.

179. *Twentieth Century Studies* (Faculty of Humanities, University of Kent at Canterbury). Issue No. 3 (May 1970) is devoted to structuralism and contains important material: e.g. Roger Poole ('Structures and

materials'), Jean-Marie Benoist ('The end of structuralism'), Todorov ('The fantastic in fiction') Geoffrey Nowell-Smith ('Cinema and structuralism'). Double issue No. 7/8 (December 1972) is devoted to Russian Formalism and includes work by Todorov ('Some approaches to Russian Formalism') Kristeva ('The ruin of a poetics') and Richard Sherwood ('Shklovsky and the development of early formalist theory of prose literature').

180. *Working Papers in Cultural Studies* (*WPCS*) published by the Centre for Contemporary Cultural Studies, University of Birmingham. *WPCS* 1 (1971) includes a translation of Barthes's 'Rhetorique de l'image'. *WPCS* 3 (1972) includes Eco's 'Towards a semiotic inquiry into the TV message' and a valuable bibliography of 'Ideological analysis of the message' by Marina de Camargo. *WPCS* 5 (1974) includes Fredric Jameson on 'The vanishing mediator: narrative structure in Max Weber'. *WPCS* 6 (1974) includes Iain Chamber's critical analysis 'Roland Barthes: structuralism/semiotics'. *WPCS* 9 (1976) includes Charles Woolfson 'The semiotics of working class speech' and Andrew Tolson 'On the semiotics of workers' speech'. The Centre for Contemporary Cultural Studies also produces a series of stencilled Occasional Papers, including a translation of Barthes's 'Introduction à l'analyse structurale des récits' (No. 6) and, earlier, Tim Moore's *Lévi-Strauss and the Cultural Sciences* as Occasional Pamphlet No. 4. This offers, in an Appendix, some 'Notes towards the analysis of the James Bond Stories' (cf. Eco and Del Buono, *The Bond Affair* in section V).

181. *Yale French Studies* Nos 36–7 (1966) were devoted to structuralism and have been published as a separate volume: see Ehrmann (ed.) section I. The journal periodically publishes relevant material, and Nos 44 and 45 both contain essays by Todorov ('Valéry's poetics' and 'The discovery of language: *Les liaisons dangereuses* and *Adolphe*' respectively).

182. Finally, two new series of volumes, ed. Thomas A. Sebeok, have recently been announced by the Research Center for Language and Semiotic Studies, Indiana University, Bloomington, Indiana: *Advances in Semiotics* (Eco's *A Theory of Semiotics*, see section V, is one of this series) and *Studies in Semiotics* (Jakobson's *Coup de l'oeil sur le developpement de la sémiotique*, see section V, appears in this series).

Some suggested reading patterns

The following sequences of reading are suggested as reasonably basic (though not exhaustive) introductions to the topics indicated, beginning with the simplest exposition and moving by degrees towards a greater complexity. Clearly, the areas covered by some of the topics will overlap and a number of items will recur in different contexts and in different patterns. To a certain degree this can be said to act as a measure of their significance. The numbers refer to the items as listed in the above bibliography.

1. *Structuralism:* (a) *Introduction for beginners:* 1; 2 (particularly the introduction); 116; 7 (particularly Lyons, Culler, Leach and Eco); 4; 22. (b) *More advanced studies:* 6; 8; 67–73.

2. *Semiotics:* (a) *Introduction for beginners:* 136; 7 (Eco); 145 (the early chapters); 148, 22; 128; 178; 165. (b) *More advanced studies:* 151; 48 (Sebeok's 'survey of the state of the art'); 129; 150; 153–4; 135; 158; 159–65; 180 (particularly *WPCS* 3, 6 and 9); 142.

3. *The anthropological basis of structuralism:* 7 (Leach); 4; 22; 25–31; 35; 50.

4. *The linguistic basis of structuralism:* 7 (Lyons, Culler); 4; 8; 15; 22; 11; 39 (Leach); 49; 41.

5. *Linguistics and anthropology:* 22; 25; 28; 27; 39 (Leach: compare the later 22); 42; 43; 51 (these last three items constitute the basis of the Sapir-Whorf 'hypothesis' concerning language and culture. See especially Steiner, 51 and compare Vico, 50.

6. *Linguistics and literature:* 39 (Steiner); 14; 23; 37; 38; 40; 47 (particularly Jakobson); 17; 20; 55; 88–91; 106; 171. And see *Jakobson* below.

7. *Formalism:* 52; 54; 53; 59; 57; 58.

8. *Structuralism and literary criticism:* 116; 4; 8; 93 (particularly the introduction); 104; 112; 94 and then compare with 78; 2 or 5 (Lévi-Strauss and Jakobson on Baudelaire) and then compare with 3 (Riffaterre); 17 (Jakobson on Shakespeare and then Richards on Jakobson); 179 (May 1970, particularly Todorov); 47 (Jakobson's 'Closing Statement') and then compare 21 and 20. As an antidote 121.

9. *Semiotics and literary criticism:* 165; 145; 143; 137; 164; 167; 136; 151.

10. *Saussure:* basic: 44; 45; more complex: 57; 92.

11. *Lévi-Strauss:* basic: 33; 35; 36; 22; more complex: 71; with Jakobson: 5.

12. *Jakobson:* basic: 18–21; more complex: 2; 5; 3 (Riffaterre); 111; 153; 154.

13. *Barthes:* basic: 84; more complex: 76; 85; 78–83. With reference to semiotics, 128 (read the amusing short studies, but 'Myth today' is basic), *followed by* the earlier 129 and 130.

14. *The Barthes-Picard debate:* 84; 87; 85; the debate itself: 75; 115; 77.

FURTHER READING (2003)

I have argued that 'classic' structuralism in literary criticism virtually ends with Roland Barthes's *S/Z* (see pp. 94–99). That book's testing, virtually to destruction, of the codes that form the basis of its own analysis more or less opened the floodgates to the deconstructive tide that followed. It also made the drawing up of a list of works for 'further' reading in respect of structuralism rather problematical. In one sense, literary structuralism went and could go no further. But of course this did not prevent a daunting number of books being written about it, including my own. *Structuralism and Semiotic*'s original Bibliography, with its sub-divisions and reading patterns, still strikes me as reasonably adequate, if by no means comprehensive. The aim of the following much more modest addition to it is briefly to draw attention to some of the salient developments in critical theory that have succeeded structuralism, in particular those which, whilst not necessarily deriving directly from its precepts, may be said to have been marked – some would say shaped – by its perceptions as well as its limitations and presuppositions. Needless to say, it is in the nature of the rapidly overlapping expansion of the subject that the sub-divisions in this case are almost wholly arbitrary.

BEYOND STRUCTURALISM

Michel Foucault, *The Archaeology of Knowledge*, trans. A. M. Sheridan Smith, London: Tavistock Publications, 1972.

—— *The Foucault Reader*, ed. Paul Rabinow, New York: Random House; Harmondsworth: Penguin Books, 1984.

John Sturrock (ed.), *Structuralism and Since: from Levi-Strauss to Derrida*, Oxford: Oxford University Press, 1979. See also the chapter on 'Post-Structuralism' in the same author's *Structuralism*, London: Grafton Books (Collins), 1986, pp. 136–65.

Josué V. Harari (ed.), *Textual Strategies: Perspectives in Post-Structuralist Criticism*, Ithaca, N.Y.: Cornell University Press, 1979; London: Methuen, 1980.

Barbara Johnson, *The Critical Difference*, Baltimore: Johns Hopkins University Press, 1981.

Robert Young (ed.), *Untying the Text: a Post-structuralist Anthology*, London: Routledge, 1981.

Richard Harland, *Superstructuralism: the Philosophy of Structuralism and Post-Structuralism*, London and New York: Methuen, 1987.

DECONSTRUCTION

Jacques Derrida, *Of Grammatology*, trans. Gayatri Chakravorty Spivak, Baltimore, Md: Johns Hopkins University Press, 1976. Derrida's analysis of Saussure (pp. 27–73) is crucial.

Jonathan Culler, *The Pursuit of Signs: Semiotics, Literature, Deconstruction*, London: Routledge; Ithaca, N.Y.: Cornell University Press, 1981.

—— *On Deconstruction: Theory and Criticism after Structuralism*, London: Routledge, 1983.

Christopher Norris, *Deconstruction: Theory and Practice* (New Accents series), London and New York, Routledge 1982. (second edition 2002).

—— *Derrida*, London: Fontana Press, 1987.

POSTMODERNISM

Jacques Lacan, *Écrits, a Selection*, trans. Alan Sheridan, London and New York: Tavistock Publications, 1977 (see also Malcolm Bowie, *Lacan*, London: Fontana Press, 1991).

—— *The Four Fundamental Concepts of Psycho-Analysis*, trans. Alan Sheridan, Harmondsworth: Penguin, 1994.

Paul de Man, *Allegories of Reading*, New Haven: Yale University Press, 1979.

—— *Blindness and Insight: Essays in the Rhetoric of Contemporary Criticism* (revised edn), London: Methuen 1983.

—— *The Resistance to Theory*, Manchester University Press, 1986.

Geoffrey Hartman, *Criticism in the Wilderness*, New Haven: Yale University Press, 1982.

Fredric Jameson, *The Political Unconscious: Narrative as a Socially Symbolic Act*, London: Routledge 1981.

—— 'Postmodernism or the Cultural Logic of Late Capitalism', *New Left Review* 146, 1984, pp. 53–93.

Hayden White, *Tropics of Discourse*, Johns Hopkins University Press, 1982.

Edward Said, *The World, the Text, and the Critic*, Cambridge, Mass.: Harvard 1983; London: Faber, 1984.

Jean-Francois Lyotard, *The Postmodern Condition*, trans. R. Durand, Manchester: Manchester University Press, 1986.

Linda Hutcheon, *A Poetics of Postmodernism*, London: Routledge, 1988.

Madan Sarup, *An Introductory Guide to Post-Structuralism and Postmodernism*, Brighton: Harvester, 1989.

Richard Rorty, *Contingency, Irony and Solidarity*, Cambridge: Cambridge University Press, 1989.

Christopher Norris, *What's Wrong with Postmodernism*, Brighton: Harvester, 1990.

—— *The Truth About Postmodernism*, Oxford: Blackwell, 1993.

Catherine Belsey, *Desire: Love Stories in Western Culture*, Oxford: Blackwell, 1994.

INDEX